AAT

Qualifications and Credit Framework (QCF)

AQ2013

LEVEL 2 CERTIFICATE IN ACCOUNTING

TEXT

Control Accounts,
Journals and the
Banking System

2014 Edition

For assessments from September 2014

Second edition June 2014
ISBN 978 1 4727 0899 1

Previous edition
ISBN 978 1 4727 0314 9

British Library Cataloguing-in-Publication Data
A catalogue record for this book is available from the British
Library

Published by
BPP Learning Media Ltd
BPP House
Aldine Place
London
W12 8AA

www.bpp.com/learningmedia

Printed in the United Kingdom by Martins of Berwick
Sea View Works
Spittal
Berwick-Upon-Tweed
TD15 1RS

Your learning materials, published by BPP Learning Media Ltd,
are printed on paper sourced from traceable sustainable sources.

CONTENTS

BPP LEARNING MEDIA'S AAT MATERIALS

The AAT's assessments fall within the **Qualifications and Credit Framework** and most papers are assessed by way of an on demand **computer based assessment**. BPP Learning Media has invested heavily to ensure our materials are as relevant as possible for this method of assessment. In particular, our **suite of online resources** ensures that you are prepared for online testing by allowing you to practise numerous online tasks that are similar to the tasks you will encounter in the AAT's assessments.

Resources

The BPP range of resources comprises:

- **Texts**, covering all the knowledge and understanding needed by students, with numerous illustrations of 'how it works', practical examples and tasks for you to use to consolidate your learning. The majority of tasks within the texts have been written in an interactive style that reflects the style of the online tasks we anticipate the AAT will set. When you purchase a Text you are also granted free access to your Text content online.

- **Question Banks**, including additional learning questions plus the AAT's sample assessment(s) and a number of BPP full practice assessments. Full answers to all questions and assessments, prepared by BPP Learning Media Ltd, are included. Our question banks are provided free of charge in an online environment containing tasks similar to those you will encounter in the AAT's testing environment. This means you can become familiar with being tested in an online environment prior to completing the real assessment.

- **Passcards**, which are handy pocket-sized revision tools designed to fit in a handbag or briefcase to enable you to revise anywhere at anytime. All major points are covered in the Passcards which have been designed to assist you in consolidating knowledge.

- **Workbooks**, which have been designed to cover the units that are assessed by way of computer based project/case study. The workbooks contain many practical tasks to assist in the learning process and also a sample assessment or project to work through.

- **Lecturers' resources**, for units assessed by computer based assessments. These provide a further bank of tasks, answers and full practice assessments for classroom use, available separately only to lecturers whose colleges adopt BPP Learning Media material.

This Text for Control Accounts, Journals and the Banking System has been written specifically to ensure comprehensive yet concise coverage of the AAT's **AQ2013** learning outcomes and assessment criteria.

Each chapter contains:

- Clear, step by step explanation of the topic

- Logical progression and linking from one chapter to the next

- Numerous illustrations of 'how it works'

- Interactive tasks within the text of the chapter itself, with answers at the back of the book. The majority of these tasks have been written in the interactive form that students can expect to see in their real assessments

- Test your learning questions of varying complexity, again with answers supplied at the back of the book. The majority of these questions have been written in the interactive form that students can expect to see in their real assessments

The emphasis in all tasks and test questions is on the practical application of the skills acquired.

Supplements

From time to time we may need to publish supplementary materials to one of our titles. This can be for a variety of reasons, from a small change in the AAT unit guidance to new legislation coming into effect between editions.

You should check our supplements page regularly for anything that may affect your learning materials. All supplements are available free of charge on our supplements page on our website at:

www.bpp.com/about-bpp/aboutBPP/StudentInfo#q4

Customer feedback

If you have any comments about this book, please email ianblackmore@bpp.com or write to Ian Blackmore, AAT Range Manager, BPP Learning Media Ltd, BPP House, Aldine Place, London W12 8AA.

Any feedback we receive is taken into consideration when we periodically update our materials, including comments on style, depth and coverage of AAT standards.

In addition, although our products pass through strict technical checking and quality control processes, unfortunately errors may occasionally slip through when producing material to tight deadlines.

When we learn of an error in a batch of our printed materials, either from internal review processes or from customers using our materials, we want to make sure customers are made aware of this as soon as possible and the appropriate action is taken to minimise the impact on student learning.

As a result, when we become aware of any such errors we will:

1) Include details of the error and, if necessary, PDF prints of any revised pages under the related subject heading on our 'supplements' page at: www.bpp.com/about-bpp/aboutBPP/StudentInfo#q4

2) Update the source files ahead of any further printing of the materials

3) Investigate the reason for the error and take appropriate action to minimise the risk of reoccurrence.

A NOTE ON TERMINOLOGY

The AAT AQ2013 standards and assessments use international terminology based on International Financial Reporting Standards (IFRSs). Although you may be familiar with UK terminology, you need to now know the equivalent international terminology for your assessments.

The following information is taken from an article on the AAT's website and compares IFRS terminology with UK GAAP terminology. It then goes on to describe the impact of IFRS terminology on students studying for each level of the AAT QCF qualification.

Note that since the article containing the information below was published, there have been changes made to some IFRSs. Therefore BPP Learning Media have updated the table and other information below to reflect these changes.

In particular, the primary performance statement under IFRSs which was formerly known as the 'income statement' or the 'statement of comprehensive income' is now called the 'statement of profit or loss' or the 'statement of profit or loss and other comprehensive income'.

What is the impact of IFRS terms on AAT assessments?

The list shown in the table that follows gives the 'translation' between UK GAAP and IFRS.

UK GAAP	IFRS
Final accounts	Financial statements
Trading and profit and loss account	Statement of profit or loss (or statement of profit or loss and other comprehensive income)
Turnover or Sales	Revenue or Sales Revenue
Sundry income	Other operating income
Interest payable	Finance costs
Sundry expenses	Other operating costs
Operating profit	Profit from operations
Net profit/loss	Profit/Loss for the year/period
Balance sheet	**Statement of financial position**
Fixed assets	Non-current assets
Net book value	Carrying amount
Tangible assets	Property, plant and equipment

UK GAAP	IFRS
Reducing balance depreciation	Diminishing balance depreciation
Depreciation/Depreciation expense(s)	Depreciation charge(s)
Stocks	Inventories
Trade debtors or Debtors	Trade receivables
Prepayments	Other receivables
Debtors and prepayments	Trade and other receivables
Cash at bank and in hand	Cash and cash equivalents
Trade creditors or Creditors	Trade payables
Accruals	Other payables
Creditors and accruals	Trade and other payables
Long-term liabilities	Non-current liabilities
Capital and reserves	Equity (limited companies)
Profit and loss balance	Retained earnings
Minority interest	Non-controlling interest
Cash flow statement	Statement of cash flows

This is certainly not a comprehensive list, which would run to several pages, but it does cover the main terms that you will come across in your studies and assessments. However, you won't need to know all of these in the early stages of your studies – some of the terms will not be used until you reach Level 4. For each level of the AAT qualification, the points to bear in mind are as follows:

Level 2 Certificate in Accounting

The IFRS terms do not impact greatly at this level. Make sure you are familiar with 'receivables' (also referred to as 'trade receivables'), 'payables' (also referred to as 'trade payables'), and 'inventories'. The terms sales ledger and purchases ledger – together with their control accounts – will continue to be used. Sometimes the control accounts might be called 'trade receivables control account' and 'trade payables control account'. The other term to be aware of is 'non-current asset' – this may be used in some assessments.

Level 3 Diploma in Accounting

At this level you need to be familiar with the term 'financial statements'. The financial statements comprise a 'statement of profit or loss' (previously known as an income statement), and a 'statement of financial position'. In the statement of profit or loss the term 'revenue' or 'sales revenue' takes the place of 'sales', and 'profit for the year' replaces 'net profit'. Other terms may be used in the statement of financial position – eg 'non-current assets' and 'carrying amount'. However, specialist limited company terms are not required at this level.

Level 4 Diploma in Accounting

At Level 4 a wider range of IFRS terms is needed, and in the case of Financial statements, are already in use – particularly those relating to limited companies. Note especially that a statement of profit or loss becomes a 'statement of profit or loss and other comprehensive income'.

Note: The information above was taken from an AAT article from the 'assessment news' area of the AAT website (www.aat.org.uk). However, it has been adapted by BPP Learning Media for changes in international terminology since the article was published and for any other changes needed.

AAT UNIT GUIDE

Control Accounts, Journals and the Banking System (CJBS)

Introduction

Please read the information below in conjunction with the standards for all relevant units.

Purpose of the Unit

The practical nature of this unit will help students develop skills that are valued in the workplace and will make students attractive to future employers.

This unit places emphasis on more complex Level 2 accounting skills which will give students the confidence they need to perform well in the workplace and prepare them for greater responsibility.

Those who have achieved this Level 2 unit will not only benefit employers through the relevant knowledge that they have acquired, but also through the practical skills they have gained, enabling them to carry out reconciliations, adjustments through the journal and banking tasks, with confidence. They will add value to a business organisation with their up to date knowledge of business practices and the motivated and willing approach that AAT students develop during the learning process.

Learning Objectives

This unit will enable students to further develop their understanding of the double entry bookkeeping system.

Students will develop the necessary knowledge and skills to use the journal to record a variety of transactions. They will need to know how to process transactions through the ledgers and carry out reconciliation of the sales and purchases ledger control accounts as well as the VAT control account.

Students will be able to redraft the initial trial balance, following adjustments. They will also understand the banking system and the importance of retaining banking documents for the required period.

The skills and knowledge detailed above are reflected in the six learning outcomes included in this unit, each of which has two or more assessment criteria:

Learning Outcomes	Covered in Chapter
LO1 Understand the purpose and use of control accounts and journals (eight assessment criteria)	2-5
LO2 Maintain and use control accounts (three assessment criteria)	2, 3
LO3 Maintain and use a journal (six assessment criteria)	4, 5
LO4 Reconcile a bank statement with the cash book (three assessment criteria)	1
LO5 Understand the banking process (six assessment criteria)	1, 6
LO6 Understand retention and storage requirements relating to banking documents (two assessment criteria)	1, 6

Guidance on delivery

This guidance is structured in skills areas relevant to control accounts, journals and the banking system and then matched to the relevant assessment criteria.

This unit requires the student to understand the double entry bookkeeping system and be able to perform double entry bookkeeping tasks.

Sales and purchases ledger control accounts will be contained in the general ledger forming part of the double entry system. The individual accounts of trade receivables and trade payables will be in the sales and purchases ledgers and will therefore be regarded as subsidiary accounts.

The six broad skills areas which will be tested are as follows:

1   Control accounts
2   The journal
3   Trial balance
4   Bank reconciliation
5   Banking system
6   Document retention

Each skills area relates to assessment criteria in one or more of the above learning outcomes.

1   CONTROL ACCOUNTS

Students will be required to understand general and specific purposes of sales and purchases ledger control accounts and the need for regular reconciliation and to deal with discrepancies quickly and professionally. They will be required to prepare, balance and reconcile sales and purchases ledger control accounts and understand the purpose of an aged trade receivables analysis.

Students will also need to understand the general and specific purpose of the VAT control account and be able to prepare and balance a VAT control account and verify the balance, for instance with the VAT return.

Assessment criteria for control accounts:

1.1 Describe the general purpose of control accounts

1.2 Describe the specific purpose of the sales ledger, purchases ledger and VAT control accounts

1.3 Explain the importance of reconciling the sales and purchases ledger control accounts regularly

1.4 Describe the purpose of an aged trade receivables analysis

1.5 Explain the need to deal with discrepancies quickly and professionally

2.1 Prepare sales ledger, purchases ledger and VAT control accounts

2.2 Reconcile sales and purchases ledger control accounts with the relevant ledgers

2.3 Verify the balance on the tax control account

2   THE JOURNAL

Students will need to understand the format and content of the journal, and be able to prepare the following journal entries:

- Opening entries for a new business or new financial year

- Irrecoverable debts written off, including VAT

- Payroll transactions including gross pay, income tax, employer's and employees' NIC, employer's and employees' pension and voluntary deductions

- Opening and clearing a suspense account

- Correcting errors not disclosed by the trial balance

- Correcting errors disclosed by the trial balance

Payroll transactions will always be recorded using a wages control account.

Errors include: errors of omission, commission, principle, original entry, reversal of entries, compensating error, calculation errors in ledger accounts, single entry transactions, recording two debits or two credits for a transaction, errors transferring balances to the trial balance or omission of a general ledger account in the trial balance.

Students will not be required to identify errors within accounting records but they must be able to deal with errors appropriately.

Students will be required to recognise types of errors by name, that is, errors of omission, commission, principle, original entry, reversal of entries, or compensating error. They must also be able to recognise whether or not a given error will cause an imbalance in the trial balance.

Students will be required to post journal entries to the general ledger accounts, including the suspense account, and understand the reasons for maintaining the journal.

Assessment criteria for the journal:

1.6 Describe the reasons for maintaining the journal

1.7 Explain the content and format of the journal

1.8 Identify errors that are corrected through the journal

3.1 Create journal entries to record a new set of double entry bookkeeping records, an irrecoverable debt written off, wages and salaries

3.2 Create journal entries to correct errors not disclosed by the trial balance

3.3 Create journal entries to open a suspense account to balance the trial balance

3.4 Create journal entries to correct errors disclosed by the trial balance and to clear the suspense account

3.5 Record journal entries in the ledger accounts

3   TRIAL BALANCE

Students must be able to balance the trial balance using a suspense account and then redraft the trial balance following the correction of errors and elimination of the suspense account. They should be able to complete trial balances that are in alphabetical order, random order or in the order of final accounts.

Assessment criteria for the trial balance:

3.3   Create journal entries to open a suspense account to balance the trial balance

3.6   Redraft the trial balance following adjustments

4   BANK RECONCILIATION

Students will need to be able to update a simple cash-book from the bank statement, and total and balance the cash-book. The updating entries may include bank interest received or paid, bank charges or automated payments and receipts.

Students must be able to prepare a bank reconciliation statement.

Assessment criteria for the bank reconciliation:

4.1   Identify differences between individual items on the bank statement and in the cash-book

4.2   Update the cash-book from the bank statement

4.3   Prepare a bank reconciliation statement

5   BANKING SYSTEM

Students should be prepared to answer a variety of questions on the banking system.

Students should understand the main services offered by banks and building societies. As many building societies are banks the distinction will be made between small mutual building societies and banks, with the former not offering corporate services.

Students will need to understand when funds banked will be available for use, which may not be immediately due to the clearing system. There is no requirement for the student to understand how the clearing system works.

Students must understand these different forms of payment: cash, cheques, credit cards, debit cards, and automated payments. They should know the checks that

should be made on cheques, credit cards and debit cards before they are accepted.

It is important that students understand the need to keep receipts and payments secure and the security procedures that should be in place.

Students should recognise that different forms of payment (cheque, credit card and debit card) will have different effects on the bank balance.

Assessment criteria for the banking system:

5.1 Identify the main services offered by banks and building societies

5.2 Explain when funds banked are cleared and available for use

5.3 Identify other forms of payment: cash, cheque, credit cards, debit cards, automated payments

5.4 Identify the information required to ensure the following payments are valid: cheque, credit card, debit card

5.5 Describe procedures to ensure the security of receipts and payments

5.6 Describe the effect that different forms of payment will have on an organisation's bank balance

6 DOCUMENT RETENTION

Students should be able to recognise banking documents that should be retained and the required retention period. They should understand the importance of an organisation's document retention policy in relation to banking and be able to answer a variety of questions on the topic.

Assessment criteria for document retention:

6.1 Explain the importance of a formal document retention policy for an organisation

6.2 Identify the different types of documents that should be stored securely

ASSESSMENT STRATEGY

Control Accounts, Journals and the Banking System (CJBS) is the second of two bookkeeping assessments at Level 2. It builds on the skills already acquired from studying Processing Bookkeeping Transactions and introduces more complex bookkeeping procedures. It takes the student through the reconciliation processes and to the stage of re-drafting the initial trial balance once adjustments through the journal have been made.

Studying this unit will provide an important foundation for the financial accounting units at Level 3.

The assessment is normally a computer based assessment (CBT) and students will be required to respond to CBT tasks in a variety of ways, for example using multiple choice, true/false, drag and drop, drop-down list, text select, linking boxes, gap fill tools and AAT purpose-built question types to reflect real workplace activities.

Assessment duration: two hours.

The CJBS assessment consists of 12 tasks in one section.

Competency

For the purpose of assessment the competency level for AAT assessment is set at 70 per cent. The level descriptor in the table below describes the ability and skills students at this level must successfully demonstrate to achieve competence.

QCF Level descriptor	**Summary**
	Achievement at Level 2 reflects the ability to select and use relevant knowledge, ideas, skills and procedures to complete well-defined tasks and address straightforward problems. It includes taking responsibility for completing tasks and procedures and exercising autonomy and judgement subject to overall direction or guidance.
	Knowledge and understanding
	■ Use understanding of facts, procedures and ideas to complete well-defined tasks and address straightforward problems.
	■ Interpret relevant information and ideas.
	■ Be aware of the types of information that are relevant to the area of study or work.
	Application and action
	■ Complete well-defined, generally routine tasks and address straightforward problems.
	■ Select and use relevant skills and procedures.
	■ Identify, gather and use relevant information to inform actions.
	■ Identify how effective actions have been.
	Autonomy and accountability
	■ Take responsibility for completing tasks and procedures.
	■ Exercise autonomy and judgement subject to overall direction or guidance.

Task	Learning outcome	Assessment criteria	Maximum marks	Title for topics within task range
1	1, 3	1.7 Implied 3.1	12	Prepare journals for opening entries
2	1, 3	1.7 Implied 3.1	12	Prepare journals for payroll transactions
3	1, 3	1.7 Implied 1.8, 3.1	14	Prepare journals for irrecoverable debts written off Identify types of error
4	1, 3	1.7 Implied 3.2	12	Prepare journals for correction of errors
5	1, 3	1.7 Implied, 1.6, 3.3, 3.4	12	Balance the trial balance and prepare journals for correction of errors
6	1, 3	1.7 Implied 3.5	12	Post journal entries to ledger accounts
7	3	3.6	14	Re-draft the trial balance
8	4	4.1, 4.2	14	Update the cash-book
9	4, 5	4.1, 4.3, 5.5	14	Prepare a bank reconciliation statement
10	1, 2	1.1 – 1.5, 2.1, 2.2	14	Prepare and reconcile sales/purchases ledger control accounts
11	1, 2	1.2, 2.1, 2.3	12	Prepare a VAT control account and verify the balance
12	5, 6	5.1 – 5.4, 5.6, 6.1, 6.2	12	Understand the banking system and the importance of document retention

chapter 1:
BANK RECONCILIATIONS

chapter coverage 📖

Nearly every organisation has an account with a bank, into which it pays cash and other payments received, and from which it authorises the bank to make payments on its behalf. The cash book is the book of prime entry in which the organisation records transactions that affect its bank account. It is particularly vital for any business to ensure control over its money held at the bank. A key means of control is through the bank reconciliation process. The topics covered are:

✍ Introduction to the cash book

✍ Transactions affecting the bank account

✍ Automated payments into and out of the bank account

✍ Bank statements

✍ Comparing the bank statement to the cash book

✍ Bank reconciliation statement

✍ Summary

INTRODUCTION TO THE CASH BOOK

The cash book is arguably the most important record maintained in an organisation's accounting system.

The cash book as a book of prime entry

The first stage of any accounting process is to enter details of transaction documents into BOOKS OF PRIME ENTRY (often known as DAY BOOKS as, in theory at least, they would be written up every day).

TRANSACTION   ⟶   BOOKS OF
DOCUMENTS   PRIME ENTRY

An organisation's CASH BOOK is the book of prime entry for **transactions affecting the balance of money held in the business's bank account**. It is also the book of prime entry for **discounts allowed** to customers and **discounts received** from suppliers.

Note that the cash book may also be used as the book of prime entry for cash transactions affecting the balance of **cash held on the premises**, that is cash received primarily in respect of cash sales and held until it is banked. (It is **never** the book of prime entry for petty cash.) Some purchases and other transactions may be paid for in the meantime out of the cash held in this way. We shall not be considering the use of the cash book for cash transactions further in this Text.

There are various transaction documents that are the primary source for recording information about bank account transactions in the cash book, as we shall see in this chapter.

The cash book as part of the double entry system

As well as being the book of prime entry for transactions affecting cash held at the bank, the cash book is also often part of an organisation's double entry system. This means that the payments side is the credit side, and the receipts side is the debit side, of the BANK ledger account.

Here is a simple example of a cash book that is also part of the double entry system.

- Items on the debit side are **receipts** into the bank account, from various persons (Dagwell, Polygon etc) in the form of cash, cheques or automated payments.

- Items on the credit side are **payments** from the bank account, to various credit suppliers (Seeban, Electricom etc) by cheque or automated payment.

- Because receipts (debits) exceed payments (credits), there is a balance carried down from the credit side to the debit side. This means there is a positive balance on the account.

Cash Book

DEBIT SIDE		CREDIT SIDE	
Details	Bank £	Details	Bank £
Bal b/f	12,940.00	Seeban	1,284.90
Dagwell	336.50	Electricom	440.00
Polygon	158.20	Comtec	650.37
Hayward	227.40	Chiller	849.37
G Thomas	269.43	Purchase by cheque	500.40
Whitehill	673.58	Benham	400.00
Weller	225.49	Gas Supplies	200.00
Treseme	2,910.00		
Cash/cheques paid in	200.00	Bal c/d	13,615.56
Totals	17,940.60	Totals	17,940.60
Bal b/d	13,615.56		

Control over the cash book's accuracy: the bank reconciliation

A bank must prepare regular statements of account or **bank statements** for its customer so the customer can check that the bank is keeping good care of its money. The bank can only include on the bank statement transactions of which it is aware, that is:

- Amounts of money received into the bank account (the bank will be able to show where the money came from, but not what it was for)
- Amounts of money paid from the bank account (the bank may be able to show who the money was paid to and how, but again not what it was for)

It is vitally important that the cash book is prepared accurately, and that as much control as possible is maintained over its accuracy. A key way to do this is to

perform regular **bank reconciliations**, in which we use the **bank statement** prepared by the bank to check that our **cash book** is complete and accurate.

In relation to the simple cash book seen earlier, we might hope to find that the balance we calculate of £13,615.56 at the particular date in question is the same balance as the bank calculates at that same date. For various reasons this will rarely be so: the bank reconciliation process is more complicated than that, as we shall see later in this chapter.

TRANSACTIONS AFFECTING THE BANK ACCOUNT

A business's bank account is affected by a variety of transactions, many of which will be familiar to you in relation to your own personal bank account:

Amounts paid in to the bank account:

- Cash paid in at the bank's counter or via an automated teller machine (ATM)

- Cheques received and paid in at the bank's counter or via an automated teller machine (ATM)

- Automated payments received

- Interest received from the bank

Amounts paid out of the bank account:

- Cheques issued to suppliers and presented by them to the bank for payment

- Debit card payments made in person, online or over the phone (note that credit card payments do not affect the bank account directly at all, as there is a separate credit card account with the credit card company)

- Automated payments paid

- Interest and bank charges paid to the bank

We shall look in more detail at cash receipts, and at cheque and debit card payments, in Chapter 6. For the moment we shall look at the various types of automated payment. In doing so we need to bear in mind that, as well as payments being made 'automatically' **out** of the bank account by the business, payments by customers and other third parties can also come **in** to the bank account automatically.

AUTOMATED PAYMENTS INTO AND OUT OF THE BANK ACCOUNT

Businesses are increasingly keen to make automated payments to their suppliers, in which case there are normally two primary records for the business receiving the payment:

- The **remittance advice note** sent by the customer, which shows the amount of the payment and any settlement discount being taken (it should also show which specific invoices are being paid).

- The business's **bank statement**, which shows the amount of the payment actually received (we shall come back to this).

In some cases, such as when a business is in regular receipt of rental income, instead of a remittance advice note there may be a **payment schedule** for perhaps the year ahead. This schedule will list out when each amount will be received into the business's bank account. The actual receipt can then be checked on the business's bank statement.

Automated payments may take one of several forms:

- A bank giro credit (BGC)
- A BACS transfer
- A CHAPS transfer
- A Faster Payment
- A standing order
- A direct debit

Bank giro credit

A BANK GIRO CREDIT (BGC) is a method by which a customer can pay a cheque (or cash) into its supplier's bank account directly rather than sending it through the post. Bank giro credit slips are often pre-printed at the bottom of invoices and statements for credit cards and for utilities such as phone, electricity etc.

HOW IT WORKS

Southfield Electrical has received an invoice for phone charges and wishes to pay this by bank giro credit.

Step 1   A cheque is written out for the amount of the invoice.

Step 2   The bank giro credit slip at the bottom of the invoice is detached and the amount of the cheque written in, together with the date and an authorised signature:

Step 3   The cheque and bank giro credit slip are handed in at Southfield's bank and the payment leaves Southfield's bank account in due course and reaches that of the phone company.

BACS transfer

BACS stands for Bankers Automated Clearing System. This is a system for making transfers between one bank account and another via the banks' computer systems. These are sometimes known as direct credits. Unlike a bank giro credit BACS means that, to make a payment to another party's bank account, there is no need to physically go to the bank itself with a cheque or cash.

For a business making payments to various recipients (suppliers, employees etc), the details of each recipient's bank account and the amount to be paid are submitted to the BACS Clearing Centre by computer. The payments are then taken directly from the business's bank account and paid in to each recipient's bank account.

The first a recipient of a payment by BACS will know about the receipt is when it appears in its bank account, unless it receives a remittance advice note separately.

CHAPS transfer

A CHAPS transfer is an instruction by a business to its bank to move money to the recipient's account at another bank so that the funds are available the same working day. Unlike with a cheque, the funds transfer is performed instantaneously so there is no chance for the business to stop the payment, and the bank cannot refuse payment once it has been made due to insufficient funds. CHAPS transfers are commonly used for large amounts such as transferring funds to solicitors for the purchase of property.

Faster Payments

Most large banks and building societies in the UK now allow their customers to make small and medium-sized payments via the internet using the Faster Payments system. The business must follow various security procedures to access its bank account online, and then to enter the recipient's details and authorise the payment. If it is for a small amount then the payment is deducted immediately from the business's account, and is available almost immediately in the recipient's account.

Standing order schedule

A STANDING ORDER is a method of making the same regular payment directly from a business's bank account to the bank account of a supplier or other third party. This is organised through the bank by filling in a STANDING ORDER SCHEDULE in paper or online – an example is shown below:

STANDING ORDER SCHEDULE

To: First National Bank

Please make the payments detailed below and debit my account:

Name of account to be debited   Southfield Electrical

Account number   _____

Payee details   _____

Name of payee   _____

Bank of payee   _____

Sort code of payee   _____

Account number of payee   _____

Amount of payment (in words)   _____ £ _____

STANDING ORDER SCHEDULE

Date of first payment   _____

Frequency of payment   _____

Continue payments until   _____

Signature   _____   Date   _____

This standing order schedule is an order to the First National Bank to make a payment of a fixed amount out of Southfield Electrical's bank account and into that of the payee on a regular basis. Security procedures must be followed and it must be authorised properly before being submitted to the bank.

The following details are included on a standing order schedule:

- It is addressed to the business's bank

- Details of the business's bank account

- Details of the payee and their bank account ie, account number, sort code, bank name

- The amount of the payment

- The date of the first payment

- The frequency of the payment thereafter, usually monthly or quarterly

- The date that the payments cease

- The authorised signatory for the account

As a standing order is for a fixed amount it is not particularly useful for paying credit suppliers, but it is often used for making fixed payments such as rent, insurance premiums or loan repayments.

Direct debits

A DIRECT DEBIT is also a method of making a payment directly from the business's bank account to that of another party. However, it operates in a different manner to a standing order, since it is activated by the recipient of the transfer and is normally for a variable amount paid at intermittent periods.

HOW IT WORKS

Suppose that Southfield Electrical wish to pay National Water for its water rates by direct debit. The steps in the process are as follows:

Step 1   National Water sends Southfield Electrical a Direct Debit mandate which it has prepared – an example is given below.

NATIONAL WATER

Please fill in the whole form including 'the official use' box using a ball point pen and send the form to us at the address below in the envelope provided. Please do not send this instruction direct to your bank.

> National Water plc
> PO Box 284
> Donchurch
> South Yorkshire
> DN4 5PE

Name(s) of Account Holder(s)

Bank/Building Society account number

Branch Sort Code

Name and full postal address of your Bank or Building Society

To: The Manager	Bank/Building Society
Address	
	Postcode

Reference Number (as shown on your water services bill)

2	2	3	0	1	7	4	0	1	2	0	1	6

DIRECT Debit

Instruction to your Bank or Building Society to pay by Direct Debit

Originator's Identification Number

6	2	4	8	3	2

FOR NATIONAL WATER PLC OFFICIAL USE ONLY
This is not part of the instruction to your Bank or Building Society
To be completed by customer
Please tick required option:

☐ Annually ☐ Half Yearly ☐ Monthly April to January

☐ 1st of the month ☐ 15th of the month

Instruction to your Bank or Building Society

Please pay National Water plc Direct Debits from the account detailed in this Instruction subject to the safeguards assured by the Direct Debit Guarantee. I understand that this Instruction may remain with National Water plc and if so, details will be passed electronically to my Bank/Building Society.

Signature(s)

Date

Banks and Building Societies may not accept Direct Debit Instructions from some types of account

The Direct Debit Guarantee

DIRECT Debit

■ This Guarantee is offered by all Banks and Building Societies that take part in the Direct Debit Scheme. The efficiency and security of the Scheme is monitored and protected by your own Bank or Building Society.

■ If the amounts to be paid or the payment dates change National Water plc will notify you 10 days in advance of your account being debited or as otherwise agreed.

■ If an error is made by National Water plc or your Bank or Building Society, you are guaranteed a full and immediate refund from your branch of the amount paid.

■ You can cancel a Direct Debit at any time by writing to your Bank or Building Society. Please also send a copy of your letter to us.

Step 2   Southfield Electrical completes the Direct Debit mandate instructing its bank to pay the amounts that National Water ask for on the dates that National Water requests payment.

Step 3   Southfield Electrical return the Direct Debit mandate to National Water who then send this to its bank.

Step 4   When a payment is required from Southfield Electrical to National Water this is requested by National Water and Southfield's bank will pay the amount requested.

The usefulness of a direct debit compared to a standing order is that:

- It can be for variable rather than fixed amounts.
- It can be used for payments to be made at varying time intervals.

Security procedures for automated and other payments

All payments made by a business, whether they are automated, in cash or by cheque, must be subject to security procedures since there is large scope for fraud or excessive spending.

- Invoices from suppliers should initially be checked for accuracy against supporting documentation (such as an order or goods received note) when they are first received and before they are recorded in the purchases day book.

- Payment of an invoice should be authorised by a separate person from the one who made the purchase or placed the order.

- Authorisation should be denoted by the person's signature or initials, on the invoice or a payment schedule.

- Large payments should be authorised by a more senior person, or by more than one person.

- All authorised documents should be retained.

BANK STATEMENTS

At regular intervals a business's bank will send out a BANK STATEMENT showing transactions on the bank account since the date of the last bank statement, and a final balance on the bank account. A business current account has many payments and receipts and so may require a weekly bank statement, whereas a deposit account with less movement may only warrant a monthly statement. Many businesses will also view their transactions and balances online.

A typical bank statement for Southfield Electrical is shown below.

STATEMENT

first national
30 High Street
Benham
Dr4 8TT

SOUTHFIELD ELECTRICAL   **Account number:** 20-26-33 40268134

CHEQUE ACCOUNT   **Sheet 023**

Date	Sheet 023	Paid out	Paid in	Balance
20XX				
17 Oct	Balance brought forward			2,595.23 C
18 Oct	Cheque No 003067	424.80		
	Cheque No 003069	122.60		2,047.83 C
19 Oct	DD Benham District Council	450.00		
	Counter credit		1,081.23	2,679.06 C
20 Oct	Cheque No 003073	1,480.20		
	Cheque No 003074	1,865.67		666.81 D
21 Oct	Counter credit		1,116.20	449.39 C
	Balance carried forward			449.39 C

D = debit; C = credit

There are various points to note about bank statements:

- Each sheet of a printed bank statement is sequentially numbered so a business can tell if any statements are missing.

- After each day's transactions the daily balance on the account is shown, which is calculated by adding the day's payments in to the previous day's balance, and deducting the day's payments out. In relation to this particular bank statement, note that on 17 October the business had a positive amount of money in the account, but because subsequent payments out exceeded this balance and the payment in, on 20 October the account went into an overdraft balance which is denoted by D (standing for Debit).

- A COUNTER CREDIT is a payment into the bank account made at the bank's counter by a person from the business handing over cash and cheques received to the bank.

- Other types of transaction may be given a code:

    - CHQ is a cheque payment from the account in the process of being paid.

- DD is a direct debit payment.
- SO or STO is a standing order payment.

■ A BACS or Faster Payments payment would be denoted as such on the statement.

You may have noticed something strange about the debit and credit terminology related to the daily balances on the bank statement.

■ A positive balance on the account is shown as a credit.
■ An overdraft balance is shown as a debit.

This is the opposite way round to the way in which debits and credits are treated in the bank account in the organisation's own books – money held by the business is a debit balance and an overdraft is a credit balance!

The reason for this is that the bank is looking at the accounting from the opposite side to how the business is looking at it. A positive balance means that the bank owes money to its customer, so the bank has a liability (a credit balance on the account). An overdraft balance means that its customer owes money to the bank, so the bank has an asset (a debit balance on the account).

Task 1

If money is paid into a newly opened bank current account this will appear on the bank statement as (please tick)

A debit balance [ ]

A credit balance [ ]

Dishonoured cheques

It is usually only by examining the bank statement that a business receives its first notice of a DISHONOURED CHEQUE. This means that the bank of the person who wrote out the cheque (the drawer) has refused to pay it, usually because the drawer has insufficient funds in their bank account to cover payment of the cheque.

There are two situations that may occur for a business:

■ A cheque that it has received from a customer and paid into its bank account may be dishonoured. In this case the original double entry was:

- Debit Bank (the cash book)

- Credit Trade receivables (or Sales/VAT if it was a cheque received in settlement of a cash sale)

On notice of dishonour these entries must be reversed:

- Credit Bank (the cash book)
- Debit Trade receivables (or Sales/VAT)

■ A cheque that it has sent to a supplier has been paid into its bank account by the supplier, but it has been dishonoured. The business would usually be informed of this by its bank by letter. In this case the original double entry was:

- Credit Bank (the cash book)

- Debit Trade payables (or Purchases/VAT if it was a cheque paid in settlement of a cash purchase)

On notice of dishonour these entries must be reversed:

- Debit Bank (the cash book)

- Credit Trade payables (or Purchases/VAT if it was a cheque paid in settlement of a cash purchase)

COMPARING THE BANK STATEMENT TO THE CASH BOOK

Checking that the entries in the cash book agree with the entries on the bank statement should only be done when all the known payments in for a period plus all the known payments out (by cheque, debit card, BACS, CHAPS, Faster Payments etc, standing order) have been entered into the cash book. As only known, specific amounts can be entered into the cash book it should be clear that what we are looking for on the bank statement are:

- Transactions which are known about (such as a regular direct debit to, say, a phone company) but where the amount is unknown

- Transactions which are not known about

Procedure for checking the bank statement to the cash book

When the bank statement for the period is received the following steps should be followed for comparison with the cash book:

Step 1   Work through all of the payments in shown on the bank statement, comparing each one to entries in the cash book on the debit side. When each receipt has been agreed to the cash book the entry on the bank statement and in the cash book should be ticked.

Step 2   Work through all of the payments out shown on the bank statement, comparing each one to entries in the cash book on the credit side. When each payment has been agreed to the cash book the entry on the bank statement and in the cash book should be ticked.

Step 3   Any unticked items on the bank statement must be checked to ensure that the bank has not made a mistake.

Step 4   If the unticked items on the bank statement are valid the bank statement can then be used to make adjusting entries in the cash book, and eventually to prepare the bank reconciliation statement.

HOW IT WORKS

Southfield's cash book, before being cast etc, for the week ending 28 September 20XX is as follows (note that transaction references, including cheque numbers, have been entered on the credit side):

Cash book

DEBIT SIDE		CREDIT SIDE		
Details	Bank £	Details	Transaction reference	Bank £
Bal b/f	12,940.00	Seeban	003102	1,284.90
Dagwell	336.50	Electricom	003103	440.00
Polygon	158.20	Comtec	003104	650.37
Hayward	227.40	Chiller	003105	849.37
G Thomas	269.43	Purchase by cheque	003106	500.40
Whitehill	673.58	Benham	STO	400.00
Weller	225.49	Gas Supplies	DD	200.00
Treseme	2,910.00			
Cash/cheques paid in	200.00			

Its bank statement for the week ending 28 September 20XX is shown below.

FIRST NATIONAL BANK

30 High Street, Benham, DR4 8TT

STATEMENT

Account Name:

Southfield Electrical Ltd

Account No: 20-26-33 40268134

Date 20XX	Details	Paid out £	Paid in £	Balance £
21/09	Balance b/f			12,940.00 C
	Counter credit		336.50	
24/09	BGC – B B Berry Ltd		442.19	13,718.69 C
	Counter credit		158.20	
	BACS transfer – Hayward		227.40	
25/09	STO – Benham District Council	400.00		13,704.29 C
27/09	Bank charges	15.80		
	Counter credit		269.43	
	Faster Payment – Whitehill		673.58	
	DD – Gas Supplies	200.00		14,431.50 C
28/09	Cheque 003102	1,284.90		
	BGC – Treseme		2,910.00	
	Cheque 003104	650.37		
	BACS – wages	1,804.80		
	BACS transfer – Weller		225.49	
	Counter credit		200.00	14,026.92 C

Now we need to compare the entries on the bank statement to the entries in the cash book.

Step 1 Compare the amounts paid in on the bank statement to the debit side. As each amount paid in on the bank statement (a further copy is shown after the cash book) is agreed to the cash book, both the cash book (debit side) and the bank statement are ticked.

Cash book

DEBIT SIDE		CREDIT SIDE		
Details	Bank £	Details	Cheque number	Bank £
Bal b/f	12,940.00	Seeban	003102	1,284.90
Dagwell	✓336.50	Electricom	003103	440.00
Polygon	✓158.20	Comtec	003104	650.37
Hayward	✓227.40	Chiller	003105	849.37
G Thomas	✓269.43	Purchase by cheque	003106	500.40
Whitehill	✓673.58	Benham DC	STO	400.00
Weller	✓225.49	Gas Supplies	DD	200.00
Treseme	✓2,910.00			
Cash/cheques paid in	✓200.00			

Step 2   Compare the payments in the bank statement to the credit side of the cash book. When each payment from the bank statement is agreed to the credit side, tick the item in both the cash book and the bank statement.

Use the descriptions of the entries and any cheque numbers to help you locate the items in the cash book.

Cash book

DEBIT SIDE		CREDIT SIDE		
Details	Bank £	Details	Cheque number	Bank £
Bal b/f	12,940.00	Seeban	003102	✓1,284.90
Dagwell	✓336.50	Electricom	003103	440.00
Polygon	✓158.20	Comtec	003104	✓650.37
Hayward	✓227.40	Chiller	003105	849.37
G Thomas	✓269.43	Purchase by cheque	003106	500.40
Whitehill	✓673.58	Benham DC	STO	✓400.00
Weller	✓225.49	Gas Supplies	DD	✓200.00
Treseme	✓2,910.00			
Cash/cheques paid in	✓200.00			

FIRST NATIONAL BANK

30 High Street, Benham, DR4 8TT

STATEMENT

Account Name:

Southfield Electrical Ltd

Account No: 20-26-33 40268134

Date 20XX	Details	Paid out £	Paid in £	Balance £
21/09	Balance b/f			12,940.00 C
	Counter credit		✓336.50	
24/09	BGC – B B Berry Ltd		442.19	13,718.69 C
	Counter credit		✓158.20	
	BACS transfer – Hayward		✓227.40	
25/09	STO – Benham District Council	✓400.00		13,704.29 C
27/09	Bank charges	15.80		
	Counter credit		✓269.43	
	Faster Payment – Whitehill		✓673.58	
	DD – Gas Supplies	✓200.00		14,431.50 C
28/09	Cheque 003102	✓1,284.90		
	BGC – Treseme		✓2,910.00	
	Cheque 003104	✓650.37		
	BACS – wages	1,804.80		
	BACS transfer – Weller		✓225.49	
	Counter credit		✓200.00	14,026.92 C

Step 3 We now need to consider the items on the bank statement that are still unticked.

Unticked items on the bank statement

Let's start with the unticked amount paid in – there is a bank giro credit receipt from B B Berry Ltd of £442.19 on 24 September which, as it is not ticked, needs to be included on the debit side of the cash book. If we were using the analysis columns of the cash book we would analyse this receipt to Trade receivables if B B Berry had a credit account with us, and would double check to see whether B B Berry had taken settlement discount when making the payment. We would find this information on the remittance advice note from B B Berry Ltd. If there was no credit account we would analyse it to Cash sales and VAT.

When this payment in has been entered into the cash book both the cash book and the bank statement should be ticked.

Cash book

DEBIT SIDE		CREDIT SIDE		
Details	Bank £	Details	Cheque number	Bank £
Bal b/f	12,940.00	Seeban	003102	✓1,284.90
Dagwell	✓336.50	Electric	003103	440.00
Polygon	✓158.20	Comtec	003104	✓650.37
Hayward	✓227.40	Chiller	003105	849.37
G Thomas	✓269.43	Cash purchase	003106	500.40
Whitehill	✓673.58	Benham DC	STO	✓400.00
Weller	✓225.49	Gas	DD	✓200.00
Treseme	✓2,910.00			
Cash sale	✓200.00			
B B Berry	✓442.19			

FIRST NATIONAL BANK

30 High Street, Benham, DR4 8TT

STATEMENT

Account Name:

Southfield Electrical Ltd

Account No: 20-26-33 40268134

Date 20XX	Details	Paid out £	Paid in £	Balance £
21/09	Balance b/f			12,940.00 C
	Counter credit		✓336.50	
24/09	BGC – B B Berry Ltd		✓442.19	13,718.69 C
	Counter credit		✓158.20	
	BACS transfer – Hayward		✓227.40	
25/09	STO – Benham District Council	✓400.00		13,704.29C
27/09	Bank charges	15.80		
	Counter credit		✓269.43	
	Faster Payment – Whitehill		✓673.58	
	DD – Gas Supplies	✓200.00		14,431.50 C
28/09	Cheque 003102	✓1,284.90		
	BGC – Treseme		✓2,910.00	
	Cheque 003104	✓650.37		
	BACS – wages	1,804.80		
	BACS transfer – Weller		✓225.49	
	Counter credit		✓200.00	14,026.92 C

Now for the payments out – there are more unticked items here:

- 27/9 Bank charges £15.80 – these have not yet been entered into the credit side of the cash book as they would only have been known about when the bank statement was received. Therefore the cash book must be adjusted to show these bank charges.

- 28/9 BACS wages payment £1,804.80 – there must have been an error in not entering this in the cash book. Southfield would have authorised and scheduled the wages payment through BACS and this should have been entered into the cash book. Again an adjustment must be made for this.

Cash book

DEBIT SIDE		CREDIT SIDE		
Details	Bank £	Details	Cheque number	Bank £
Bal b/f	12,940.00	Seeban	003102	✓1,284.90
Dagwell	✓336.50	Electricom	003103	440.00
Polygon	✓158.20	Comtec	003104	✓650.37
Hayward	✓227.40	Chiller	003105	849.37
G Thomas	✓269.43	Purchase by cheque	003106	500.40
Whitehill	✓673.58	Benham DC	STO	✓400.00
Weller	✓225.49	Gas Supplies	DD	✓200.00
Treseme	✓2,910.00	Bank charges		✓15.80
Cash/cheques paid in	✓200.00	Wages	BACS	✓1,804.80
B B Berry	✓442.19			

FIRST NATIONAL BANK

30 High Street, Benham, DR4 8TT

STATEMENT

Account Name:

Southfield Electrical Ltd

Account No: 20-26-33 40268134

Date 20XX	Details	Paid out £	Paid in £	Balance £
21/09	Balance b/f			12,940.00 C
	Counter credit		✓336.50	
24/09	BGC – B B Berry Ltd		✓442.19	13,718.69C
	Counter credit		✓158.20	
	BACS transfer – Hayward		✓227.40	
25/09	STO – Benham District Council	✓400.00		13,704.29C
27/09	Bank charges	✓15.80		
	Counter credit		✓269.43	
	Faster Payment – Whitehill		✓673.58	
	DD – Gas Supplies	✓200.00		14,431.50C
28/09	Cheque 003102	✓1,284.90		
	BGC – Treseme		✓2,910.00	
	Cheque 003104	✓650.37		
	BACS – wages	✓1,804.80		
	BACS transfer – Weller		✓225.49	
	Counter credit		✓200.00	14,026.92 C

The bank charges and wages are ticked in both the cash book and the bank statement when they have been entered into the cash book.

Every item on the bank statement has now been ticked.

You will note, however, that there are still three unticked items in the credit side of the cash book. These are cheques that have been written and sent out to each supplier but that have not yet been presented for payment by the supplier, and have therefore not been paid out of Southfield's bank account. These are known as UNPRESENTED CHEQUES and will be dealt with later in the chapter.

Other possible discrepancies

So far we have discovered from the bank statement a bank giro credit paid in that was not recorded in the debit side of the cash book, and bank charges and a BACS payment paid out that were not recorded in the credit side of the cash book.

There are a few other types of difference that might be discovered:

- **Bank interest received** – some bank accounts earn interest when there is a positive balance on the account and therefore, instead of bank charges, there might be a payment in of bank interest being added to the balance on the bank account.

- **Standing order or direct debit** – we saw earlier that the standing order and direct debit schedules should be consulted when writing-up the cash book and any known automated payments out for the period put through. However if this procedure was omitted, if the direct debits are for variable amounts or if a new standing order or direct debit was not included in the schedule, then the bank statement would be the first evidence of the payment out.

- **BACS or Faster Payments** – any payment out using BACS or the Faster Payments service is authorised by the business and therefore should be written up in the cash book immediately, but if this procedure is ignored then the bank statement may be the first record of it. It is more likely in fact that payments in made by customers using BACS or Faster Payments will not be known about until the bank statement arrives, at which point they should be entered in the debit side of the cash book.

- **Bank errors** – banks do make errors and, in particular, you must check carefully the amount and date of payment of standing orders and direct debits, and the validity of any automated payments and receipts.

- **Dishonoured cheque paid in** – as we saw earlier, sometimes the business will not actually receive the money from a cheque it has paid in as it is returned by the customer's bank. This might be due either to the fact that the customer has 'stopped' or cancelled the cheque or because the cheque has 'bounced' or been returned 'refer to drawer' (the 'drawer' is the customer, that is the person who wrote out the cheque), usually because the customer has insufficient funds in its account. In either case the money will not be received on this cheque

and an adjustment is required in the cash book. The adjustment is made by crediting the cash book, debiting either Trade receivables or Sales/VAT. The entries on the bank statement for a dishonoured – sometimes called a 'returned' – cheque from a supplier would appear as follows:

FIRST NATIONAL BANK
30 High Street, Benham, DR4 8TT

STATEMENT
Account Name:
Southfield Electrical Ltd
Account No: 20-26-33 40268134

Date 20XX	Details	Paid out £	Paid in £	Balance £
1/10	Counter credit		160.00	
7/10	Cheque returned unpaid	160.00		

- **Dishonoured cheque paid out** – if the business sends out a cheque that its bank refuses to pay, this may not appear on the bank statement at all, if the bank simply does not process the payment. Alternatively the payment may appear as a 'paid out' item on the bank statement, and then shortly afterwards appear as a 'paid in' item. This means the bank is 'writing back' or reversing the payment. The business still needs to adjust its cash book however once either the bank or the supplier inform it of a problem. The entry will be to debit the cash book and to credit Trade payables or Purchases/VAT. Note that a well-run business should not send a cheque which will be dishonoured, since this incurs administrative costs within the business, a fee from the bank and a bad reputation with its supplier.

Task 2

If a figure for bank interest appeared in the paid in column of the bank statement, this would be adjusted for in the (please tick)

Debit side of the cash book	
Credit side of the cash book	

Task 3

A standing order from the standing order schedule has been omitted from the cash book. This should be adjusted for in the (please tick)

Debit side of the cash book ☐

Credit side of the cash book ☐

BANK RECONCILIATION STATEMENT

We can now recalculate the balance on Southfield Electrical's cash book as at 28 September 20XX:

Cash book

DEBIT SIDE		CREDIT SIDE		
Details	Bank £	Details	Cheque number	Bank £
Bal b/f	12,940.00	Seeban	003102	✓1,284.90
Dagwell	✓336.50	Electricom	003103	440.00
Polygon	✓158.20	Comtec	003104	✓650.37
Hayward	✓227.40	Chiller	003105	849.37
G Thomas	✓269.43	Purchase by cheque	003106	500.40
Whitehill	✓673.58	Benham DC	STO	✓400.00
Weller	✓225.49	Gas Supplies	DD	✓200.00
Treseme	✓2,910.00	Bank charges		✓15.80
Cash/cheques paid in	✓200.00	Wages	BACS	✓1,804.80
B B Berry	✓442.19	Balance c/d		12,237.15
Total	18,382.79	Total		18,382.79

The correct, adjusted balance for the bank account in the cash book at 28 September of £12,237.15. However, if you return to the bank statement you will see that this does not agree with the bank's closing balance of £14,026.92!

This will nearly always be the case and the reasons are TIMING DIFFERENCES. There is a time lag between recording payments into and payments out of the cash book and their appearance on the bank statement.

Cheques paid in as counter credits at the bank are recorded in the debit side of the cash book but there can be a three-day delay, caused by the banks' clearing system, before they appear on the bank statement as payments in. These are known as OUTSTANDING LODGEMENTS.

When cheques are issued to suppliers they are entered into the credit side of the cash book immediately. The cheques are then sent to the suppliers, the suppliers must take them to the bank and then there is the three-day clearing period before they appear as payments out on the bank statement. Those cheque payments that are in the cash book but not on the bank statement yet are known as UNPRESENTED CHEQUES, as we saw earlier.

We shall look in a little more detail at the banks' clearing system in Chapter 6 of this Text.

HOW IT WORKS

We can now produce a BANK RECONCILIATION STATEMENT for Southfield which will reconcile the correct, adjusted cash book balance for the bank account on 28 September with the bank statement balance on the same date.

We start with the bank statement balance.

Bank reconciliation statement at 28 September 20XX

	£	£
Balance per bank statement		14,026.92

By examining the debit side of the cash book we can see that there are no unticked items and therefore no outstanding lodgements, but there are still three unticked items on the credit side, which are unpresented cheques. If they had been presented they would have made the bank statement balance smaller, so we deduct these in the bank reconciliation statement in order to come back to the cash book balance for the bank account of £12,237.15.

Bank reconciliation statement at 28 September 20XX

	£	£
Balance per bank statement		14,026.92
Less unpresented cheques		
003103	440.00	
003105	849.37	
003106	500.40	
Total to subtract		(1,789.77)
Balance as per adjusted cash book		12,237.15

SUMMARY

We will now just summarise the procedure for carrying out a bank reconciliation before working through a further example.

Step 1   Compare the debit side of the cash book to the paid in amounts shown on the bank statement – for each paid in amount that agrees, tick the item in both the cash book and the bank statement.

Step 2   Compare the credit side of the cash book to the paid out amounts shown on the bank statement – for each paid out amount that agrees, tick the item in both the cash book and the bank statement.

Step 3   Any unticked items on the bank statement (other than errors made by the bank) are items that should have been entered into the cash book but have been omitted for some reason. Enter these into the cash book and then the adjusted balance on the cash book can be calculated as usual.

Step 4   Finally, any unticked items in the cash book are timing differences – outstanding lodgements (debit side) and unpresented cheques (credit side) – that are used to reconcile the bank statement closing balance to the correct, adjusted cash book closing balance.

HOW IT WORKS

Given below is a summary of the cash book of a sole trader, Dawn Fisher, for February.

Cash book – debit side

Date	Details	Bank £
2 Feb	Balance b/f	387.90
2 Feb	G Hollings	1,368.48
7 Feb	S Dancer	368.36
14 Feb	K C Ltd	2,004.37
20 Feb	F W Painter	856.09
26 Feb	J J Hammond	648.34
28 Feb	L Minns	257.50
		5,891.04

Note that Dawn pays in each cheque at her bank as it is received.

Cash book – credit side

Date	Details	Cheque number	£
3 Feb	Long Associates	103567	1,007.46
5 Feb	Harland Bros	103568	524.71
5 Feb	L and P Timms	103569	1,035.76
8 Feb	Peter Thomas	103570	663.45
15 Feb	Gas Supplies	103571	480.50
20 Feb	F P Travel	103572	1,233.80
24 Feb	K Riley	103573	246.58
26 Feb	Farman Ltd	103574	103.64
			5,295.90

Dawn has just received her bank statement for the month of February.

STATEMENT

first national
30 High Street
Benham
DR48TT

DAWN FISHER   **Account number**: 20-26-33 40268134

CHEQUE ACCOUNT   **Sheet 011**

Date		Paid out £	Paid in £	Balance
1 Feb	Balance b/f			387.90 C
6 Feb	Counter credit		1,368.48	1,756.38 C
9 Feb	Cheque No 103568	524.71		1,231.67 C
11 Feb	Counter credit		368.36	
	Bank giro credit		208.34	
	Cheque No 103567	1,107.46		700.91 C
13 Feb	Cheque No 103570	663.45		37.46 C
18 Feb	Counter credit		2,004.37	
	SO – FC Property	400.00		1,641.83 C
19 Feb	Cheque No 103571	480.50		1,161.33 C
24 Feb	Counter credit		856.09	
	Cheque No 103569	1,035.76		981.66 C
28 Feb	Bank interest		4.84	986.50 C
28 Feb	Balance c/f			986.50 C

The bank reconciliation will now be prepared:

- Compare the debit and credit entries in the cash book to the amounts paid in and out on the bank statement – for each one that agrees, tick both the bank statement and the cash book entry.

Cash book – debit side (compare with paid in column on the bank statement)

Date	Details	Bank £	
2 Feb	Balance b/f	387.90	
2 Feb	G Hollings	1,368.48	✓
7 Feb	S Dancer	368.36	✓
14 Feb	K C Ltd	2,004.37	✓
20 Feb	F W Painter	856.09	✓
26 Feb	J J Hammond	648.34	
28 Feb	L Minns	257.50	
Total		5,891.04	

Cash book – credit side (compare with paid out column on the bank statement)

Date	Details	Cheque number	Bank £	
3 Feb	Long Associates	103567	1,007.46	
5 Feb	Harland Bros	103568	524.71	✓
5 Feb	L and P Timms	103569	1,035.76	✓
8 Feb	Peter Thomas	103570	663.45	✓
15 Feb	Gas Supplies	103571	480.50	✓
20 Feb	F P Travel	103572	1,233.80	
24 Feb	K Riley	103573	246.58	
26 Feb	Farman Ltd	103574	103.64	
Total			5,295.90	

STATEMENT

first national
30 High Street
Benham
DR48TT

DAWN FISHER   **Account number**: 20-26-33 40268134

CHEQUE ACCOUNT   **Sheet 011**

Date		Paid out £	Paid in £	Balance
1 Feb	Balance b/f			387.90 C
6 Feb	Counter credit		1,368.48✓	1,756.38 C
9 Feb	Cheque No 103568	524.71✓		1,231.67 C
11 Feb	Counter credit		368.36✓	
	Bank giro credit		208.34	
	Cheque No 103567	1,107.46		700.91 C
13 Feb	Cheque No 103570	663.45✓		37.46 C
18 Feb	Counter credit		2,004.37✓	
	SO – FC Property	400.00		1,641.83 C
19 Feb	Cheque No 103571	480.50✓		1,161.33 C
24 Feb	Counter credit		856.09✓	
	Cheque No 103569	1,035.76✓		981.66 C
28 Feb	Bank interest		4.84	986.50 C
28 Feb	Balance c/f			986.50 C

- Deal with each of the unticked items in the bank statement:

   Paid out amounts

   – Cheque number 103567 has been recorded in the credit side of the cash book as £1,007.46 whereas the bank statement shows it as an amount of £1,107.46. Assuming this is correct, the cash book must be adjusted by including an extra £100 in the credit side.

   – The standing order of £400.00 on 18 February has not been recorded in the credit side of the cash book, so it must be corrected.

Paid in amounts

- The bank giro credit of £208.34 on 11 February has not been recorded in the debit side of the cash book, so this must be corrected.

- On 28 February an amount of £4.84 bank interest was paid in to the account by the bank account – this must be entered into the debit side of the cash book.

■ Adjust the cash book to find the corrected bank balance. Tick the items as they are written in to tie up with the bank statement. The items that remain unticked in the cash book are timing differences that will appear on the bank reconciliation, so it is good practice to mark these items in the cash book with an R (for 'reconciling').

Cash book – debit side

Date	Details	Bank £	
2 Feb	Balance b/f	387.90	
2 Feb	G Hollings	1,368.48	✓
7 Feb	S Dancer	368.36	✓
14 Feb	K C Ltd	2,004.37	✓
20 Feb	F W Painter	856.09	✓
26 Feb	J J Hammond	648.34	R
28 Feb	L Minns	257.50	R
11 Feb	BGC	208.34	✓
28 Feb	Bank interest received	4.84	✓
Total		6,104.22	

Cash book – credit side

Date	Details	Cheque number	Bank £	
3 Feb	Long Associates	103567	1,007.46	✓
5 Feb	Harland Bros	103568	524.71	✓
5 Feb	L and P Timms	103569	1,035.76	✓
8 Feb	Peter Thomas	103570	663.45	✓
15 Feb	Gas Supplies	103571	480.50	✓
20 Feb	F P Travel	103572	1,233.80	R
24 Feb	K Riley	103573	246.58	R
26 Feb	Farman Ltd	103574	103.64	R
11 Feb	Correction of cheque	103567	100.00	✓
18 Feb	FC Property	STO	400.00	✓
28 Feb	Bal c/d		308.32	
Total			6,104.22	

- Now the bank statement balance must be reconciled with this adjusted balance on the cash book – this is done by listing the items marked 'R' in the cash book as the reconciling items (timing differences).

Bank reconciliation statement at 28 February 20XX

	£	£
Balance per bank statement		986.50
Add outstanding lodgements (from debit side)		
J J Hammond	648.34	
L Minns	257.50	
Total to add		905.84
		1,892.34
Less unpresented cheques (from credit side)		
103572	1,233.80	
103573	246.58	
103574	103.64	
Total to subtract		(1,584.02)
Balance as per correct, adjusted cash book		308.32

The bank statement and the cash book have now been reconciled and the figure that will appear in the trial balance for the Bank account is the correct, adjusted cash book balance of £308.32.

Task 4

A cheque in the credit side of the cash book is unticked after the bank statement and cash book have been compared.

How should this be dealt with in the bank reconciliation statement?

As an unpresented cheque ☐

As an outstanding lodgement ☐

Opening balances on the cash book and bank statement

In both examples you may have noted that the opening balance (balance b/f) on the cash book was the same as that on the bank statement – this means there were no unpresented cheques or outstanding lodgements at the end of the previous period.

This will not always be the case. If there were timing differences at the end of the previous period then you would have prepared a bank reconciliation statement at that date. When comparing this period's bank statement and cash book you therefore need to have the previous period's bank reconciliation statement to hand in order to tick off last period's timing differences when they appear on the bank statement in this period.

HOW IT WORKS

When Dawn is preparing her bank reconciliation at the end of March she will find that the unpresented cheques at the end of February, cheque numbers 103572 to 103574, appear on the bank statement in March. When they are found on the bank statement in March then they should be ticked on that bank statement and on the opening bank reconciliation statement. The same will happen with the two outstanding lodgements at the end of February when they appear on the bank statement in March. As they are timing differences there is no question of making any adjustment in the cash book.

Task 5

A business's bank statement shows bank charges paid out. This has not been recorded in the cash book.

How would this be recorded in the bank ledger account?

Debit

Credit

Overdraft balances

Take care when calculating the balance on the cash book to identify whether its opening balance is a debit balance (often called CASH AT BANK on a trial balance) or a credit balance – an OVERDRAFT.

HOW IT WORKS

Suppose that the opening balance on Southfield's cash book on 2 May was a credit balance of £225.68. The total receipts for the week ending 9 May are £4,246.73 and the total payments £4,114.98. What is the closing balance on the cash book?

As the opening balance is an overdraft it appears on the credit side of the cash book.

	£
Opening balance (balance b/f on the credit side)	(225.68)
Total bank payments for week	(4,114.98)
Total bank receipts for week	4,246.73
Closing balance (balance c/d on the debit side)	(93.93)

Task 6

The opening overdrawn balance on a business's cash book is £1,367.34. Amounts paid in for the period are £7,336.49 and amounts paid out for the period are £4,527.22.

What is the closing balance on the cash book?

£		overdraft/ debit balance

CHAPTER OVERVIEW

- The cash book is the book of prime entry for transactions that affect the organisation's balance on its bank account

- In many organisations, the cash book acts as the Bank ledger account as well as acting as a book of prime entry

- To ensure the accuracy of the cash book, it must be checked at regular intervals to bank statements received

- The balances on the bank statement are the opposite to those in the bank ledger account as the bank is considering the accounting from its own perspective

- When checking the bank statement to the cash book, check each of the amounts paid in to and out of the bank account as shown on the bank statement to the debit and credit sides of the cash book respectively, and tick each agreed item in both the cash book and the bank statement

- Any valid unticked items on the bank statement must be entered into the cash book, as either debits or credits

- Unticked items in the cash book are timing differences (outstanding lodgements on the debit side, and unpresented cheques on the credit side) which are used to prepare the bank reconciliation statement

- Once the relevant adjustments have been made to the cash book, the cash book must be balanced

- If the opening balance on the cash book is an overdraft then this is brought forward on the credit side

- The closing balance on the bank statement is reconciled to the correct, adjusted closing cash book balance in the bank reconciliation statement. The reconciling items are the outstanding lodgements and unpresented cheques in the cash book

Keywords

BACS (Bankers Automated Clearing System) – a system for making payments directly between bank accounts

Bank Giro Credit (BGC) – payment method whereby a customer pays a cheque directly into the supplier's bank account rather than sending it through the post

Bank ledger account – the ledger account in the general ledger that contains all the transactions affecting the organisation's bank account. Usually the Bank ledger account is the cash book itself

Bank reconciliation statement – a statement reconciling the bank statement balance on a given date to the correct, adjusted cash book balance on the same date

Bank statement – shows payments into and out of the bank account since the date of the last bank statement

Books of prime entry – the books in which the details of the organisation's transactions are initially recorded prior to entry into the ledger accounts

Cash at bank – debit balance in cash book (term used in trial balance)

CHAPS – an instruction by the business to its bank to move a large amount of money to the recipient's account at another bank so the money is available the same working day

Counter credit – a term used on bank statements to refer to cash and cheques paid in to the business's bank account at the bank's counter by someone from the business

Day books – another name for books of prime entry

Direct debit – a method of making payments direct from the bank where payments are for variable amounts and/or varying time intervals

Dishonoured cheque – a cheque that has not been paid as expected by the bank on which it is drawn

Faster Payments – a system used by the major UK banks which allows customers to make small and medium-sized payments online almost instantaneously

Outstanding lodgements – cheques that have been received and recorded on the debit side of the cash book but that do not yet appear on the bank statement

Overdraft – this is where the business effectively owes the bank money – it appears as a debit balance in the bank statement and a credit balance in the cash book

Standing order – method of making regular payments directly from the bank account of the customer to the bank account of the supplier

Standing order schedule – listing showing all of the standing order payments that a business has

Timing differences – the reasons why the bank statement balance rarely agrees with the balance on the cash book, as receipts and payments recorded in the cash book appear later on the bank statement due to how the clearing system operates

Unpresented cheques – cheque payments that have been recorded in the credit side of the cash book but that do not yet appear on the bank statement

TEST YOUR LEARNING

Test 1

You are the cashier for Thames Traders and you have on your desk lists for the week ending 30 November showing cheques received and cheques sent, plus the standing order schedule. Each of these documents is reproduced below.

LIST OF CHEQUES RECEIVED FROM CREDIT CUSTOMERS			
	SL code	Amount £	Discount allowed £
Burser Ltd	SL14	147.89	6.49
Crawley Partners	SL23	448.36	18.79
Breon & Co	SL15	273.37	
Kogart Supplies	SL06	552.68	42.67
Alex & Bros	SL09	273.46	
Minicar Ltd	SL22	194.68	

	LIST OF CHEQUES SENT TO CREDIT SUPPLIERS			
		PL code	Amount £	Discount received £
001367	Waterloo Partners	PL21	336.47	12.47
001368	Central Supplies	PL16	169.36	
001369	General London Trade	PL23	268.38	10.58
001370	Eye of the Tiger	PL19	84.50	
001371	Chare & Cope	PL27	447.39	19.86

Extract from standing order schedule

27th of each month – standing order to Loan Finance Repayment Reference ML 23 £250.00

Write up the cash book for all these bank transactions.

Cash book – debit side

Date	Details	Ref	Discounts allowed £	Bank £	Trade receivables £

Cash book – credit side

Date	Details	Ref	Discounts received £	Bank £	Trade payables £	Sundry £

Test 2

You are now given the bank statement for Thames Traders for the week ending 30 November. Compare this to the cash book.

Make a note of the treatment required in either the cash book or the bank statement for any items that cannot be agreed.

STATEMENT

NATIONAL DIRECT

THAMES TRADERS

CHEQUE ACCOUNT

Account number: 15-20-40 10267432

Date	Sheet 136	Paid out	Paid in	Balance
23.11	Balance brought forward			1489.65 C
26.11	Bank Giro Credit - Burser Ltd		52.00	1541.65 C
27.11	SO-Loan Finance Repayment	250.00		1291.65 C
28.11	Cheque No 001367 Counter credit	336.47	147.89	1103.07 C
29.11	Cheque No 001368 Counter credit	196.36	448.36	1355.07 C
30.11	Counter credit Bank charges	34.53	552.68	1,873.22 C

Test 3

Adjust the cash book for any items that appear to be relevant (assume that the bank statement is correct) and total it.

Test 4

You discover from the records of Thames Traders that the debit balance on the cash book at 23 November was £1,489.65.

What figure will appear in the trial balance for the bank account at 30 November?

£ [   ]

Test 5

Reconcile the closing bank statement balance to the corrected cash book balance for Thames Traders.

	£
Balance per bank statement	
Add:	
Total to add:	
Less:	
Total to subtract:	
Balance as per correct, adjusted cash book	

Test 6

On 26 February Bremner Ltd received the following bank statement from Northpoint Bank as at 23 February.

Assume today's date is 28 February.

<table>
<tbody>
<tr><td colspan="6" style="text-align:center">Northpoint Bank PLC
17 Market Square, Axford, AX56 2HJ</td></tr>
<tr><td colspan="6">To: Bremner Ltd   Account No 92382222   23 February 20XX</td></tr>
<tr><td colspan="6" style="text-align:center">Statement of Account</td></tr>
</tbody>
</table>

Date 20XX	Detail	Paid out £	Paid in £	Balance £	
03 Feb	Balance b/f			6,230	C
03 Feb	Cheque 003252	2,567		3,663	C
03 Feb	Cheque 003253	333		3,330	C
03 Feb	Cheque 003254	1,006		2,324	C
04 Feb	Cheque 003257	3,775		1,451	D
09 Feb	BGC Branthill Co		1,559	108	
11 Feb	Cheque 003255	966		858	D
13 Feb	DD AxDC	250		1,108	D
18 Feb	DD Trust Insurance	325		1,433	D
20 Feb	Bank charges	14		1,447	D
22 Feb	Interest charge	56		1,503	D
23 Feb	Counter credit		2,228	725	C

D = Debit C = Credit   BGC = Bank Giro Credit   DD = Direct Debit

The cash book as at 23 February is shown below.

(a) Check the items on the bank statement against the items in the cash book.

(b) Using the picklist below for the details column, enter any items in the cash book as needed.

(c) Total the cash book and clearly show the balance carried down at 23 February and brought down at 24 February.

(d) Identify the four transactions that are included in the cash book but missing from the bank statement, and complete the bank reconciliation statement as at 23 February using the picklist.

Cash book

Date 20XX	Details	Bank £	Date 20XX	Cheque number	Details	Bank £
01 Feb	Balance b/f	6,230	01 Feb	003252	Jeggers Ltd	2,567
20 Feb	Straightens Co	2,228	01 Feb	003253	Short & Fell	333
21 Feb	Plumpers	925	01 Feb	003254	Rastop Ltd	1,006
22 Feb	Eastern Supplies	1,743	01 Feb	003255	A & D Trading	966
			02 Feb	003256	Jesmond Warr	2,309
			02 Feb	003257	Nistral Ltd	3,775
			13 Feb	003258	Simpsons	449
			13 Feb		AxDC	250

Bank reconciliation statement as at 23 Feb 20XX

Balance per bank statement		£	
Add:			
Name:		£	
Name:		£	
Total to add		£	
Less:			
Name:		£	
Name:		£	
Total to subtract		£	
Balance as per cash book		£	

Picklist:

A & D Trading
AxDC
Balance b/d
Balance c/d
Bank charges
Branthill Co
Closing balance
Eastern Supplies
Interest charge
Jeggers Ltd
Jesmond Warr
Nistral Ltd
Opening balance
Plumpers
Rastop Ltd
Short & Fell
Simpsons
Straightens Co
Trust Insurance

chapter 2:
INTRODUCTION TO CONTROL ACCOUNTS

―――――― **chapter coverage** 📖 ――――――

In this chapter we look first at the overall purpose of control accounts and at the three most important control accounts: trade receivables, trade payables and VAT. We then revise the postings to the sales ledger, purchases ledger and VAT control accounts and to the relevant accounts in the subsidiary sales and purchases ledger. The topics covered are:

✐ The purpose of control accounts

✐ Types of control account

✐ The accounting system for trade receivables

✐ The accounting system for trade payables

✐ The accounting system for VAT

THE PURPOSE OF CONTROL ACCOUNTS

The double entry in the general ledger for transactions relating to a business's credit sales and purchases is as follows:

- Totals for all the numerous individual credit sales and purchases transactions in the various day books were posted to 'control' accounts for the sales and purchases ledgers in the general ledger, and it was in this ledger that the other sides of the transactions were posted.

- Individual transactions were entered from the various day books into separate accounts for individual credit customers (trade receivables) in the sales ledger, and for individual credit suppliers (trade payables) in the purchases ledger.

Once all the ledger accounts – in both the general ledger and the subsidiary ledgers – are balanced then we should have:

- Balances for total trade receivables and total trade payables in the general ledger, from the two control accounts.

- Balances for individual trade receivables and trade payables in the subsidiary ledgers, which are essentially a breakdown of each total in the general ledger.

The control account system therefore means that:

- Transactions posted to the general ledger are kept to a minimum so there is less room for error in the general ledger double entry system.

- It is easy at any point in time to identify from the general ledger how much in total the business owes and is owed.

- It is possible at any point in time to see in the subsidiary ledgers how much is owed by individual trade receivables and to individual trade payables.

- The accuracy of the general ledger and the subsidiary ledgers can be checked by reconciling the balance on the control account in the former to the total of the balances on the latter (we see how to do this in Chapter 3). This helps us to identify and deal with discrepancies quickly.

TYPES OF CONTROL ACCOUNT

CONTROL ACCOUNTS for trade receivables (the sales ledger control account) and for trade payables (the purchases ledger control account) operate as a form of control over the balances owed by the many trade receivables and to the many trade payables that a business may have.

In addition there are three other types of control account that are often seen:

- Cash control and Bank control accounts – used where the cash book is just a book of prime entry, so total receipts and total payments are posted to the Cash control and the Bank control accounts at the same time as the postings are made from the analysis and discounts columns. It is on these general ledger accounts that a balance can be calculated (as a book of prime entry the cash book would not contain balances).

- Petty cash control account – again this is used where the petty cash book is just a book of prime entry, and it operates in the same way as the Cash and Bank control accounts. Again, it is on this account that a balance can be calculated (as a book of prime entry the petty cash book would not contain a balance).

- VAT control account – this is the account to which output and input VAT, plus payments to and from the UK tax collecting authority, HM Revenue & Customs (HMRC), are posted. It is on this account that a balance of VAT owed to HMRC or refundable by HMRC is calculated.

- Like the Cash, Bank and Petty cash control accounts, the VAT control account does not 'control' the accuracy of subsidiary ledgers in the same way as the sales and purchases ledgers are 'controlled' by their control accounts.

- Unlike the Cash, Bank and Petty cash control accounts however the business has no option but to maintain a VAT control account: HMRC require it. It cannot be replaced by day books doubling up as general ledger accounts.

For the rest of this chapter we shall concentrate on how the control account system operates for trade receivables, trade payables and VAT.

THE ACCOUNTING SYSTEM FOR TRADE RECEIVABLES

The process of accounting for trade receivables is as follows:

- **Sales invoices** are sent to credit customers and recorded in the sales day book.

- The total of the sales day book is debited to the sales ledger control account in the general ledger.

- The total from each individual sales invoice in the sales day book is debited to the relevant individual trade receivables' accounts in the sales ledger.

- **Credit notes** sent to customers are recorded in the sales returns day book.

- The total of the sales returns day book is credited to the sales ledger control account in the general ledger.

- The total from each individual credit note is credited to the individual trade receivables' accounts in the sales ledger.

- **Receipts** from trade receivables are debited in the cash book (debit side) and analysed under Trade receivables.

- The total of the Trade receivables column in the cash book is credited to the sales ledger control account in the general ledger.

- Each individual receipt is credited to the individual trade receivables' accounts in the sales ledger.

- **Discounts allowed** to trade receivables are recorded in the cash book (debit side).

- The total of the discounts allowed column in the cash book is credited to the sales ledger control account in the general ledger, and debited to the discounts allowed account.

- Each individual discount is credited to the individual trade receivables' accounts in the sales ledger.

HOW IT WORKS

Ben Charles has recently set up in business and he currently has just three credit customers: A, B and C. He operates both a general ledger and a sales ledger. His sales day book and cash book (debit side) for the month of May are given (he has no sales returns day book):

Sales Day Book

Date	Customer	Invoice no.	Ref	Total £		VAT £	Net £
3/05	A	0045	SL01	240.00		40.00	200.00
5/05	C	0046	SL03	144.00		24.00	120.00
8/05	B	0047	SL02	180.00		30.00	150.00
15/05	C	0048	SL03	264.00		44.00	220.00
20/05	B	0049	SL02	120.00		20.00	100.00
28/05	A	0050	SL01	216.00		36.00	180.00
				1,164.00		194.00	970.00

The total of the invoice totals (£1,164.00) must be debited to the sales ledger control account and the individual invoice totals must be debited to the individual trade receivables' accounts in the sales ledger:

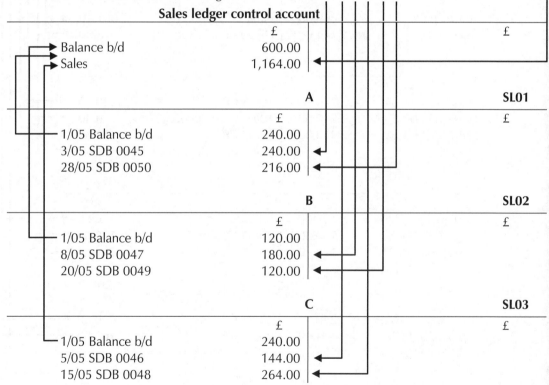

Sales ledger control account

	£		£
Balance b/d	600.00		
Sales	1,164.00		

A   **SL01**

	£		£
1/05 Balance b/d	240.00		
3/05 SDB 0045	240.00		
28/05 SDB 0050	216.00		

B   **SL02**

	£		£
1/05 Balance b/d	120.00		
8/05 SDB 0047	180.00		
20/05 SDB 0049	120.00		

C   **SL03**

	£		£
1/05 Balance b/d	240.00		
5/05 SDB 0046	144.00		
15/05 SDB 0048	264.00		

Cash Book – Debit Side

Date	Details	Ref	Bank £	Trade receivables £	Discounts allowed £
6/05	B	SL02	120.00	120.00	
10/05	A	SL01	230.60	230.60	9.40
13/05	C	SL03	200.00	200.00	
20/05	A	SL01	230.60	230.60	9.40
28/05	C	SL03	100.00	100.00	
30/05	B	SL02	180.00	180.00	
			1,061.20	1,061.20	18.80

This must now also be posted to the general ledger and the sales ledger.

Sales ledger control account

	£		£
Balance b/d	600.00	Bank	1,061.20
Sales	1,164.00	Discounts allowed	18.80

A   SL01

	£		£
1/05 Balance b/d	240.00	10/05 CB	230.60
3/05 SDB 0045	240.00	10/05 CB – discount	9.40
28/05 SDB 0050	216.00	20/05 CB	230.60
		20/05 CB – discount	9.40

B   SL02

	£		£
1/05 Balance b/d	120.00	6/05 CB	120.00
8/05 SDB 0047	180.00	30/05 CB	180.00
20/05 SDB 0049	120.00		

C   SL03

	£		£
1/05 Balance b/d	240.00	13/05 CB	200.00
5/05 SDB 0046	144.00	28/05 CB	100.00
15/05 SDB 0048	264.00		

Finally, at the end of May each of the accounts should be balanced:

Sales ledger control account

	£		£
Balance b/d	600.00	Bank	1,061.20
Sales	1,164.00	Discounts allowed	18.80
		Balance c/d	684.00
	1,764.00		1,764.00
Balance b/d	684.00		

	A		SL01
	£		£
1/05 Balance b/d	240.00	10/05 CB	230.60
3/05 SDB 0045	240.00	10/05 CB – discount	9.40
28/05 SDB 0050	216.00	20/05 CB	230.60
		20/05 CB – discount	9.40
		Balance c/d	216.00
	696.00		696.00
Balance b/d	216.00		

	B		SL02
	£		£
1/05 Balance b/d	120.00	6/05 CB	120.00
8/05 SDB 0047	180.00	30/05 CB	180.00
20/05 SDB 0049	120.00	Balance c/d	120.00
	420.00		420.00
Balance b/d	120.00		

	C		SL03
	£		£
1/05 Balance b/d	240.00	13/05 CB	200.00
5/05 SDB 0046	144.00	28/05 CB	100.00
15/05 SDB 0048	264.00	Balance c/d	348.00
	648.00		648.00
Balance b/d	348.00		

Balances carried down

Note how the total of each of the individual trade receivable balances equals the balance on the sales ledger control account.

	£
A	216.00
B	120.00
C	348.00
Sales ledger control account balance	684.00

BPP
LEARNING MEDIA

If the double entry in the general ledger and the entries in the subsidiary ledger have all been correctly carried out, the total of the list of trade receivable balances in the sales ledger will always equal the balance on the sales ledger control account.

This whole process of accounting for credit sales in the general ledger and in the sales ledger, ignoring credit notes for now, can be illustrated in a diagram:

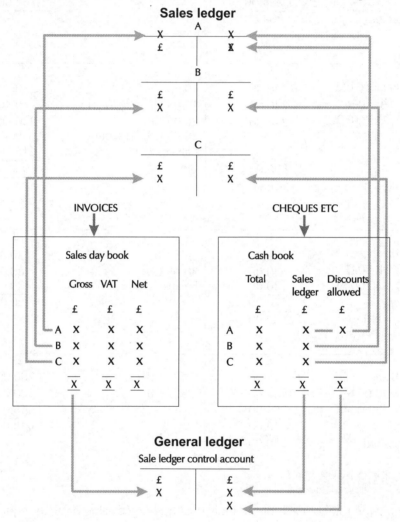

Task 1

What is the double entry in the general ledger for sales on credit?

Debit [   ]

Credit [   ]

THE ACCOUNTING SYSTEM FOR TRADE PAYABLES

The accounting process for trade payables is precisely the same as for trade receivables except that the entries in the accounts are the other way around.

- **Purchase invoices** received are recorded in the purchases day book.

- The total of the purchases day book is credited to the purchases ledger control account in the general ledger.

- Each individual invoice in the purchases day book is credited to the individual trade payables' accounts in the purchases ledger.

- **Credit notes** from trade payables are recorded in the purchases returns day book.

- The total of the purchases returns day book is debited to the purchases ledger control account in the general ledger.

- Each individual credit note is debited to the individual trade payables' accounts in the purchases ledger.

- **Payments** to trade payables are recorded in the cash book (credit side) and analysed to the trade payables column.

- The total of the trade payables column in the cash book is debited to the purchases ledger control account in the general ledger.

- Each individual payment is debited to the individual trade payables' accounts in the purchases ledger.

- **Discounts received** from trade payables are recorded in the cash book (credit side).

- The total of the discounts received column in the cash book is debited to the purchases ledger control account in the general ledger, and credited to the discounts received account.

- Each individual discount is debited to the individual trade payables' accounts in the purchases ledger.

Again this can be shown in a diagram, ignoring credit notes once again:

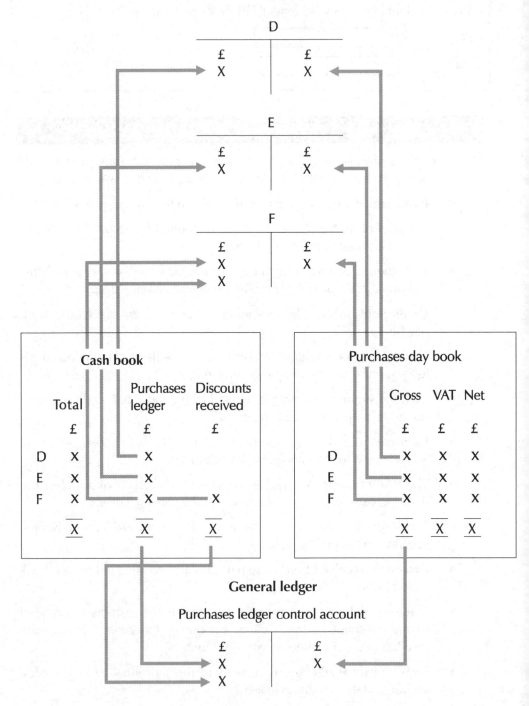

Purchases ledger

Balances carried down

In just the same way as with the accounting system for trade receivables, if the double entry has been correctly performed in the general ledger and the entries have been correctly made in the subsidiary ledger, the balances carried down on the individual trade payable accounts in the purchases ledger should total back to the balance carried down on the purchases ledger control account in the general ledger.

HOW IT WORKS

If Ben Charles has three credit suppliers, D, E and F, then the sum of the final balances on their accounts in the purchases ledger should agree with the purchases ledger control account:

D

	£		£
		Balance b/d	115.60

E

	£		£
		Balance b/d	220.00

F

	£		£
		Balance b/d	150.00

Purchases ledger control account

	£		£
		Balance b/d	485.60

	£
D	115.60
E	220.00
F	150.00
Purchases ledger control account balance	485.60

Task 2

What is the double entry in the general ledger for purchases on credit?

Debit

Credit

THE ACCOUNTING SYSTEM FOR VAT

VAT is a tax on consumers that is collected on behalf of HM Revenue & Customs (HMRC) by VAT registered businesses. At the end of each three month period the business will usually pay over to HMRC the excess of VAT collected from customers (known as output VAT) over the amount of VAT paid to suppliers (input VAT). If the business paid more VAT to suppliers than it collected from customers it will receive a refund from HMRC of the excess VAT paid.

Output and input VAT is accounted for at the same time as we account for trade receivables and trade payables respectively, but we must also account for payments of VAT owed to HMRC and refunds of VAT from them:

- The VAT amounts on sales and purchase invoices and credit notes, and on cash sales and purchases, are recorded in the day books and then totals are posted to the VAT control account.

- Payments to HMRC in respect of VAT owed is credited to the cash book and debited to the VAT control account.

- Receipts of VAT refunds from HMRC are debited to the cash book and credited to the VAT control account.

- The balance on the VAT control account is the amount owed to (credit balance) or refundable by (debit balance) HMRC.

CHAPTER OVERVIEW

- Cash, Bank and Petty cash control accounts in the general ledger are only used in businesses where the cash book and petty cash book operate as books of prime entry only

- The sales ledger control account in the general ledger is debited with sales invoices from the sales day book and credited with credit notes from the sales returns day book, and receipts and settlement discounts allowed from the cash book (debit side)

- The individual accounts for each trade receivable in the sales ledger are also debited with each invoice total and credited with the credit notes, receipts and discounts

- If all of the entries are correctly carried out then the total of the closing balances on the individual trade receivables' accounts from the sales ledger should agree to the balance on the sales ledger control account in the general ledger

- The same system applies to accounting for trade payables, although the entries are all on the opposite sides

- The VAT control account is used for all transactions (cash and credit) related to VAT, and allows the business to identify clearly how much is owed to HM Revenue & Customs in respect of VAT in a period, or how much is due from them

Keyword

Control accounts – general ledger accounts that include totals for the books of prime entry. These give no indication of individual balances

TEST YOUR LEARNING

Test 1

Assuming they all include VAT where relevant, identify the double entry for the following transactions.

	Bank DR/CR	SLCA DR/CR	PLCA DR/CR	VAT DR/CR	Sales DR/CR	Purchases returns DR/CR	Discounts received DR/CR	Discounts allowed DR/CR
Gross sales								
Gross purchases returns								
Discounts allowed								
Discounts received								
Gross payments from cash customers								
Payments to credit suppliers								

Test 2

DP Printing is a small company that currently has only four credit customers. The opening balances on the trade receivables' accounts in DP's sales ledger at the start of May 20XX were as follows:

	£
Virgo Partners	227.58
McGowan & Sons	552.73
J J Westrope	317.59
Jacks Ltd	118.36

The opening balance on the sales ledger control account at the start of May was £1,216.26.

2: Introduction to control accounts

The business banks cheques received in respect of cash sales immediately. The Sales Day Book and Cash Book (debit side) for May are given below:

Sales Day Book

Date	Customer	Total £	VAT £	Net £
3 May	J J Westrope	167.40	27.90	139.50
10 May	Virgo Partners	96.72	16.12	80.60
12 May	Jacks Ltd	107.64	17.94	89.70
15 May	J J Westrope	277.32	46.22	231.10
20 May	McGowan & Sons	595.08	99.18	495.90
23 May	Jacks Ltd	177.60	29.60	148.00
30 May	Virgo Partners	214.44	35.74	178.70
		1,636.20	272.70	1,363.50

Cash Book – Debit Side

Date	Details	Discounts allowed £	Bank £	VAT £	Cash sales £	Trade receivables £
4 May	Cash sales		486.96	81.16	405.80	
4 May	Virgo Partners		117.38			117.38
10 May	Cash sales		451.80	75.30	376.50	
12 May	J J Westrope	8.73	308.86			308.86
15 May	McGowan & Sons		552.73			552.73
17 May	Cash sales		512.28	85.38	426.90	
20 May	Jacks Ltd		100.00			100.00
30 May	Cash sales		582.24	97.04	485.20	
		8.73	3,112.25	338.88	1,694.40	1,078.97

(a) Write up the sales ledger control account for the month and the individual trade receivables' accounts in the sales ledger.

(b) Agree the control account balance to the total of the sales ledger account balances at the end of the month.

General ledger

Sales ledger control account

	£		£

BPP
LEARNING MEDIA

61

Sales ledger

Virgo Partners

	£		£

McGowan & Sons

	£		£

J J Westrope

	£		£

Jacks Ltd

	£		£

Reconciliation

	£
Sales ledger control account balance as at 31 May	
Total of sales ledger accounts as at 31 May	
Difference	

Test 3

DP Printing has three credit suppliers and the opening balances on its trade payables' accounts in the purchases ledger at the start of May were:

	£
Jenkins Suppliers	441.56
Kilnfarm Paper	150.00
Barnfield Ltd	247.90

The opening balance on the purchases ledger control account at the start of May was £839.46.

The business pays for cash purchases by cheque. The purchases day book and cash book (credit side) for the period are given below:

Purchases Day Book

Date	Supplier	Total £	VAT £	Net £
5 May	Kilnfarm Paper	153.12	25.52	127.60
10 May	Jenkins Suppliers	219.96	36.66	183.30
12 May	Barnfield Ltd	317.16	52.86	264.30
20 May	Kilnfarm Paper	153.12	25.52	127.60
27 May	Jenkins Suppliers	451.32	75.22	376.10
30 May	Barnfield Ltd	312.24	52.04	260.20
		1,606.92	267.82	1,339.10

Cash Book – Credit Side

Date	Details	Discount received £	Bank £	VAT £	Cash purchases £	Trade payables £
5 May	Cash purchases		230.52	38.42	192.10	
10 May	Jenkins Suppliers	17.67	423.89			423.89
12 May	Kilnfarm Paper		150.00			150.00
15 May	Cash purchases		321.84	53.64	268.20	
20 May	Barnfield Ltd	12.40	235.50			235.50
27 May	Kilnfarm Paper		150.00			150.00
30 May	Cash purchases		214.92	35.82	179.10	
		30.07	1,726.67	127.88	639.40	959.39

(a) Write up the purchases ledger control account for May and the individual trade payables' accounts in the purchases ledger.

(b)   Agree the control account balance at the end of May to the total of the list of individual balances in the purchases ledger.

General ledger

Purchases ledger control account

	£		£

Purchases ledger

Jenkins Suppliers

	£		£

Kilnfarm Paper

	£		£

Barnfield Ltd

	£		£

Reconciliation

	£
Purchases ledger control account balance as at 31 May	
Total of purchases ledger accounts as at 31 May	
Difference	

chapter 3:
PREPARING AND RECONCILING CONTROL ACCOUNTS

chapter coverage 📖

In this chapter we cover in more detail how to prepare control accounts using the books of prime entry, and how to reconcile them to the subsidiary ledgers. In the process we consider how to account for irrecoverable debts in regard to trade receivables, and how to use an aged trade receivables analysis. The topics covered are:

✍ Entries in the sales ledger control account

✍ Sales ledger control account reconciliation

✍ The aged trade receivables analysis

✍ Entries in the purchases ledger control account

✍ Purchases ledger control account reconciliation

✍ Entries in the VAT control account

ENTRIES IN THE SALES LEDGER CONTROL ACCOUNT

We now look in more detail at the figures that are likely to appear in the sales ledger control account, as so far we have only considered the basic entries for invoices, credit notes, payments received and discounts allowed.

A typical sales ledger control account (SLCA) might have the following types of entry:

Sales ledger control account

	£		£
Balance b/f	X	Credit sales returns	X
Credit sales	X	Payments received	X
Dishonoured cheques	X	Discounts allowed	X
		Irrecoverable debts written off	X
		Balance c/d	X
	X		X
Balance b/f	X		

These entries need a little more explanation:

Balance b/f – the brought forward balance on the account at the beginning and at the end of the period is a (large) debit balance as credit customers owe the business money. In some circumstances an individual credit customer may have a credit balance at the start of the period, for instance if they overpay their account, but the SLCA is a total account for all trade receivables and therefore has a debit balance.

Credit sales – this is the total figure that is posted from the total column in the Sales Day Book. The credit entry is to Sales, and also to VAT control.

Dishonoured cheques – if a customer pays for goods then the SLCA is credited with the payment. If the bank then returns the cheque as unpaid, ie the cheque has been dishonoured, the original entry must be reversed by debiting the SLCA. The credit entry is in the cash book (credit side).

Credit sales returns – this is the posting of the total column in the sales returns day book. The debit entry is to Sales returns, and also to VAT control.

Payments received – this is the posting from the trade receivables column total in the cash book (debit side). The debit entry is in the cash book (debit side).

Discounts allowed – this is the posting from the discounts allowed column in the cash book (debit side). The debit entry is in the Discounts allowed account.

Irrecoverable debts written off – when a sale is made on credit to a customer it is assumed that the customer will eventually pay the amount due. However, on occasion, it may become clear that a customer is not going to pay the amount owing, because they have become insolvent or have simply disappeared. Whatever the reason, if it is thought that the customer will not pay then this is

known as an IRRECOVERABLE DEBT. Such a debt has to be removed from the ledger accounts in a process known as WRITING OFF.

Balance c/d – the closing balance on the SLCA is carried down from the credit side.

Accounting for irrecoverable debts

The accounting treatment for an irrecoverable debt is to remove it from the accounting records as it is no longer a valid trade receivable. The double entry in the general ledger is:

DR   Irrecoverable debts (an expense account) with the net amount of the sale. This debit entry must be made to the irrecoverable debts account, **not** to the sales account

DR   VAT control account with the VAT element of the debt

CR   SLCA with the invoice total (the individual sales ledger account must also be credited with the invoice total)

The trade receivable for the full, VAT-inclusive amount is removed by crediting the SLCA. The lost sale is treated as an expense of the business, by debiting the net amount to the separate irrecoverable debts expense account: the debit entry is never made in the sales account even though the effect is to reverse the sale. The VAT element of the original invoice is removed by debiting the VAT control account.

Task 1

What is the double entry for writing off an irrecoverable debt?

Debit   [   ]

Debit   [   ]

Credit   [   ]

SALES LEDGER CONTROL ACCOUNT RECONCILIATION

If all the double entry in the general ledger, and entries in the sales ledger, are correctly carried out, then the totals of the balances on the sales ledger should be equal to the balance on the control account.

Control account balance

The balance on the SLCA is the figure that will appear in the trial balance for trade receivables so it is important to ensure that the figure is correct. This is done by carrying out a SALES LEDGER CONTROL ACCOUNT RECONCILIATION.

This reconciliation compares:

- The balance on the control account with
- The total of the balances of the individual accounts in the sales ledger.

If the two totals are not the same then there are discrepancies and errors that have arisen EITHER in the control account OR in the sales ledger OR both. These must be discovered, investigated and corrected.

Errors in the double entry in the general ledger affect the control account. Errors when posting entries to the individual accounts in the sales ledger, or when calculating and listing the balances in the sales ledger, affect the list of sales ledger balances.

Errors affecting the control account

Typical errors in the double entry in the general ledger include the following:

- The books of prime entry have been added up wrongly (either undercast or overcast) so the incorrect total is entered in the control account.

- Entries have been made to the wrong side of the control account.

- The discounts allowed recorded in the cash book may be incorrectly entered.

- An irrecoverable debt may not have been recorded in the general ledger although it was written off in the sales ledger.

Sales ledger balances

Each individual account in the sales ledger must be balanced for the reconciliation to go ahead. The types of transaction that affect these accounts are exactly the same as we saw above for the control account, including irrecoverable debts and dishonoured cheques. An added complication is that there may be some credit customers who end up as trade payables rather than trade receivables because they have a credit balance on their sales ledger account rather than a debit balance. Possible reasons for credit balances in the sales ledger might be:

- If by mistake the customer paid too much for the goods owing. This would then turn them from being a trade receivable into being a trade payable ie the business owes the money back to the customer

- If the customer had returned goods after paying for them then the credit note would create a credit balance on the account, as the business owes the cost of the returned goods back to the customer

When listing out the balances on the sales ledger in order to total them and reconcile them to the SLCA, it is very important to clearly mark credit balances, so they are deducted from the total.

Errors affecting the list of sales ledger balances

Some errors do not affect the double entry in the general ledger but mean either that the individual balances in the sales ledger are not correct, or that these balances are listed and totalled incorrectly. Typical of these are:

- An entry from the books of prime entry not entered in the sales ledger at all

- Entries made to the wrong side of the sales ledger account

- An entry made as the wrong amount to the sales ledger account

- A balance on an account in the sales ledger included in the list of balances as the wrong amount or as the wrong type of balance eg a debit rather than a credit balance.

Task 2

If the sales day book total for a week is overcast by £1,000 this would affect (please tick)

The sales ledger control account

The individual accounts in the sales ledger

Preparing the sales ledger control account reconciliation

The sales ledger control account reconciliation should be carried out on a regular basis, usually monthly, so that errors and discrepancies can be identified and dealt with quickly.

HOW IT WORKS

Southfield Electrical is carrying out its sales ledger control account reconciliation at the end of October 20XX. The debit balance on the sales ledger control account is £14,382.

Sales ledger control account

	£		£
Balance b/f	14,382		

The total of the list of trade receivables account balances from the sales ledger comes to £13,777.

Step 1 Calculate the difference between the control account balance and the total of the sales ledger balances.

	£
Control account balance	14,382
Total of the list of balances	13,777
Difference	605

This difference must be investigated.

Step 2 Check the control account and the individual accounts and balances and note any errors or omissions.

In Southfield's case the following errors were noted:

(a) The trade receivables column in the cash book had been overcast by £100.

(b) The total from the sales day book for a week had been posted as £3,675 instead of £3,765.

(c) An irrecoverable debt of £240 had been written off in the individual sales ledger account but not in the general ledger.

(d) An invoice to Weller Enterprises for £478 had been entered into the account of Dagwell Enterprises instead.

(e) A cash receipt from B B Berry Ltd had been entered into the account in the sales ledger as £256 instead of the correct figure from the cash book of £265.

(f) A balance of £604 on one sales ledger account had been omitted from the list of balances.

(g) A credit balance of £20 on a sales ledger account had been included in the list of sales ledger balances as a debit balance.

Step 3   The sales ledger control account must be adjusted for any of the errors that affect it:

Sales ledger control account

	£		£
Balance b/f	14,382		
(a) Bank	100	(c) Irrecoverable debts	240
(b) Sales	90	Balance c/d	14,332
	14,572		14,572
Balance b/f	14,332		

(a)   The total from the trade receivables column in the cash book would have been credited to the sales ledger control account. Therefore if it was overcast by £100 the SLCA must be debited with £100, to reduce the amount of the original entry.

(b)   The total from the sales day book is debited to the sales ledger control account. The original entry was for £90 too little (£3,675 instead of £3,765) so an extra debit entry of £90 is required to correct the error.

(c)   To write off an irrecoverable debt the sales ledger control account must be credited as the debt is no longer receivable.

Therefore the amended net balance on the control account is £14,332.

Step 4   Adjust the total of the list of balances from the sales ledger by adding or deducting the errors that affect this total.

	£
Original total	13,777
Less additional cash receipt (265–256) (e)	(9)
Add balance omitted (f)	604
Less credit balance included as debit balance (g)	(40)
	14,332

(d)   The two sales ledger accounts will need to be adjusted in the sales ledger to correct the error but this type of error does not affect the overall total of the balances on the sales ledger accounts.

(e)   The additional receipt of £9 that should have been recorded will be recorded on the credit side of the individual ledger account and so reduces the total of the sales ledger balances.

(f)   The balance omitted must be added in to the total of the list of balances.

(g)   The £20 credit balance that was included as a debit balance would have reduced the total balance if it had been correctly included – however, twice the amount of the balance must be deducted as the balance has not been omitted but included on the wrong side and this must be cancelled out.

The amended total of the list of balances now agrees to the amended sales ledger control account total and the general ledger and sales ledger are therefore reconciled.

Task 3

If the total of the discounts allowed column from the cash book of £300 was not posted for a period, this would be adjusted for in the sales ledger control account reconciliation by adding £300 to/subtracting £300 from the sales ledger control account balance/the list of ledger balances.

THE AGED TRADE RECEIVABLES ANALYSIS

All businesses need cash in order to survive and so they are keen to monitor their trade receivables and make sure that customers who bought on credit pay what is owed when, or even before, it is due. (This is the purpose after all of allowing settlement discount; although the discount is an expense to the business, it helps to ensure that the debt is not only settled but is settled early.)

The business can easily tell from the sales ledger that a particular customer owes, say, £1,000 as that is the balance on their account. What the balance alone does not tell the business is how 'old' that debt is. If the sale was recent then the business will be unconcerned that there is a trade receivable for £1,000. If the sale took place six months ago then the business would be very worried at the 'age' of the debt, and may have cause to doubt whether it will be paid at all. It may be an irrecoverable debt.

These are aspects of what is known as 'cash management and credit control' and they are covered in detail elsewhere in your studies. One aspect is relevant here however: the AGED TRADE RECEIVABLES ANALYSIS. For CJBS you do not need to be able to prepare an aged trade receivables analysis, simply to understand how to use one in monitoring trade receivables.

Once all the correcting entries have been made in the sales ledger, it is common practice to produce an aged trade receivables analysis in the form of a schedule showing, for each trade receivable, how long the balance has been unpaid.

HOW IT WORKS

Given below is an extract from the aged trade receivables analysis for Southfield Electrical at 31 October 20XX. In it, each balance is split as follows:

- The part of each balance that is analysed as 'current' are invoices etc that have been sent out in the last 30 days (the credit period offered by Southfield) and so are 'not yet due' for payment.

- All the other analysis columns represent invoices etc that are 'overdue', in this case being two (30–59 days), three (60–89 days) or more than three (>90 days) months old.

AGED TRADE RECEIVABLES ANALYSIS						
Date: 31 October 20XX						
		BALANCE	ANALYSIS			
Customer code	Account name		Current	30–59 days	60–89 days	> 90 days
		£	£	£	£	£
SL03	Polygon Stores	2,593.29	2,593.29	0.00	0.00	0.00
SL15	Dagwell Ent	2,254.67	1,356.26	898.41	0.00	0.00
SL18	Weller Ent	2,154.72	1,118.36	637.28	399.08	0.00
SL30	G Thomas & Co	3,425.47	3,116.35	0.00	0.00	309.12
		10,428.15	8,184.26	1,535.69	399.08	309.12

The aged trade receivables analysis can be used to monitor these trade receivables and to decide whether any specific action needs to be taken with respect to chasing any customer for outstanding payments. Note the analysis is NOT sent to the business's credit customers.

- Polygon Stores – the entire balance is current which shows that Polygon is a regular payer of the amounts due within the stated 30-day credit period.

- Dagwell Enterprises – although some of the debt owed by Dagwell is current there is a large amount of £898.41 which has been outstanding for more than 30 days. It may be that Dagwell always pays in this manner or, if not, the 30–59 day amount may need to be investigated and a telephone call made or letter sent to chase Dagwell Enterprises for payment.

- Weller Enterprises – as well as the current element some of this balance is more than 60 days old and some is more than 30 days old. Southfield should write to Weller Enterprises chasing payment of the overdue amounts.

- G Thomas & Co – the vast majority of this balance is current with only a fairly small amount more than 90 days old. This old debt should be investigated as there may be a problem with the invoice or goods – perhaps G Thomas & Co returned these goods and are still awaiting a credit note.

ENTRIES IN THE PURCHASES LEDGER CONTROL ACCOUNT

A typical purchases ledger control account (PLCA) will look like this:

Purchases ledger control account

	£		£
Credit purchases returns	X	Balance b/f	X
Payments to suppliers	X	Credit purchases	X
Discounts received	X		
Balance c/d	X		
	X		X
		Balance b/f	X

Credit purchases returns – this is the posting of the total column from the purchases returns day book.

Payments to suppliers – this is the posting from the trade payables column total in the credit side of the cash book.

Discounts received – this is the posting from the discounts received column total in the cash book.

Balance c/d – the closing balance on the account is carried down from the debit side.

Balance b/f – the balance brought forward at the beginning of the period and again at the end will be on the credit side of the account. Occasionally, there may be a small debit balance brought forward on an individual account with a supplier in the purchases ledger because of items such as over-payment, but the total PLCA will always have a credit balance.

Credit purchases – this is the posting from the total column in the purchases day book.

PURCHASES LEDGER CONTROL ACCOUNT RECONCILIATION

A purchases ledger control account reconciliation works in exactly the same manner and for the same purpose as a sales ledger control account reconciliation, although there will **not** be complications related to:

- Dishonoured cheques (we will assume that our business does not write out cheques that the bank does not honour!) or

- Irrecoverable debts written off

If all the double entry in the general ledger, and entries in the purchases ledger, are correctly carried out, the totals of the balances on the purchases ledger should be equal to the balance on the control account in the general ledger.

Like the sales ledger, the purchases ledger control account reconciliation should be completed regularly, at least every month.

Control account balance

The balance on the purchases ledger control account is the figure that will appear in the trial balance for trade payables so it is important to ensure that it is correct, by carrying out a PURCHASES LEDGER CONTROL ACCOUNT RECONCILIATION.

The reconciliation compares the balance on the control account with the total of the balances of the individual accounts in the purchases ledger. If the two totals are not the same then there are discrepancies and errors that must be discovered, investigated and corrected in EITHER the control account OR the purchases ledger or both.

Errors affecting the control account

Typical types of error in the double entry in the general ledger include the following:

- The books of prime entry have been added up wrongly (either undercast or overcast) so the incorrect total is entered in the control account.

- Entries have been made to the wrong side of the control account.

- The discounts received recorded in the cash book may be incorrectly entered.

Purchases ledger balances

Each individual account in the purchases ledger must be balanced for the reconciliation to go ahead. The types of transaction that affect these accounts are exactly the same as we saw above for the control account. An added complication is that there may be some credit suppliers who end up as trade receivables rather than trade payables because they have a debit balance on their purchases ledger account rather than a credit balance. Possible reasons for debit balances in the purchases ledger may be:

- The business paid too much for the goods owing so the supplier owes the money back to the business.

- The business returned goods after paying for them and the credit note then created a debit balance on the account, as the supplier owed the cost of the returned goods back to the business.

When listing out the balances on the purchases ledger in order to total them and reconcile them to the PLCA, it is very important to clearly mark any debit balances, so they are deducted from the total.

Errors affecting the list of purchases ledger balances

Some errors do not affect the double entry in the general ledger but mean either that the individual balances in the purchases ledger are not correct, or that these balances are listed and totalled incorrectly. Typical of these are:

- An entry from the books of prime entry not entered in the purchases ledger at all.

- An entry from the books of prime entry made to the wrong account in the purchases ledger.

- Entries made in the wrong side of a purchases ledger account.

- An entry made as the wrong amount in a purchases ledger account.

- A balance on an account in the purchases ledger included in the list of balances as the wrong amount or as the wrong type of balance, eg a credit rather than a debit balance.

Task 4

If the purchases day book total for a week is undercast by £800 this would affect (please tick)

The purchases ledger control account

The individual accounts in the purchases ledger

HOW IT WORKS

Whitehill Superstores is currently preparing its purchases ledger control account reconciliation at the end of October 20XX. The balance on the purchases ledger control account is £17,240 and the total of the list of balances on the purchases ledger is £16,720.

The following discrepancies have been noted:

(a)   One page of the Purchases Day Book has been overcast by £200.

(b)   An invoice has been posted to an individual account in the purchases ledger as £957 instead of the correct figure from the Purchases Day Book of £597.

(c)   The total for discounts received of £250 has been credited to the purchases ledger control account.

(d)   One of the credit balances in the purchases ledger has been included in the total at a figure of £468 instead of £648.

Step 1   Amend the control account balance for any errors that affect it.

Purchases ledger control account

	£		£
(a) Purchases	200	Balance b/f	17,240
(c) Discounts received	250		
Discounts received	250		
Balance c/d	16,540		
	17,240		17,240
		Balance b/f	16,540

(a)   The total from the purchases day book is credited to the purchases ledger control account, and therefore if it was overcast by £200 then the PLCA must be debited by £200.

(c)   The discounts received should have been debited to the PLCA – instead they were credited and therefore there should be two debits in the PLCA for £250, one to cancel out the credit and one to make the debit entry.

Step 2   Amend the total of the list of balances to adjust for any errors that affect the individual balances or their total.

	£
Original total	16,720
(b) Less invoice misposting (957 – 597)	(360)
(d) Add balance misstated (648 – 468)	180
	16,540

(b) An invoice would be posted to the credit side of a purchases ledger account – in this case it was posted at a figure £360 too high and therefore the purchases ledger balances will be reduced when the account is amended.

(d) The balance that was misstated was shown as £180 too little – therefore the balances need to be increased by £180.

Task 5

An invoice for £200 was entered into an individual account in the purchases ledger on the wrong side of the account. This would be adjusted for in the purchases ledger control account reconciliation by

| adding £400 to/ subtracting £400 from |

| the purchases ledger control account/the list of purchases |

| ledger balances |.

ENTRIES IN THE VAT CONTROL ACCOUNT

We will now look in more detail at the figures that appear in the VAT CONTROL ACCOUNT.

A typical VAT control account for a business which owes VAT to HM Revenue & Customs (HMRC) will receive postings from more books of prime entry than either the sales or the purchases ledger control accounts, as follows:

VAT control account

	£		£
VAT on credit purchases	X	Balance b/f (owing to HMRC)	X
VAT on cash purchases	X	VAT on credit sales	X
VAT on petty cash purchases	X	VAT on cash sales	X
VAT on sales returns	X	VAT on purchases returns	X
VAT on irrecoverable debts written off	X	VAT on the sale of assets owned for several years	X
VAT paid to HMRC	X	VAT refunded by HMRC	X
Balance c/d (owing to HMRC)	X̱		
	X̱		X̱
		Balance b/f	X

- **VAT on credit purchases** – this is the VAT from the Purchases Day Book. It represents input VAT incurred on purchases which is recoverable from HMRC.

- **VAT on cash purchases** – this is the VAT from the analysis column of the cash book (credit side). It represents input VAT incurred on purchases which is recoverable from HMRC.

- **VAT on petty cash purchases** – this is the VAT from the petty cash book (credit side). It represents input VAT incurred on purchases made from petty cash which is recoverable from HMRC.

- **VAT on sales returns** – this is the VAT from the sales returns day book.

- **VAT on irrecoverable debts written off** – this is the VAT element of the amount that is written off by crediting the sales ledger control account. The remainder of the debit entry is to the irrecoverable debts expense account.

- **VAT paid to HMRC** – this is the amount that settles what the business owes to HMRC because output VAT exceeds input VAT (as it very often does). It is entered from the Cash Book (credit side). The amount due at the time a VAT RETURN is prepared for HMRC is the balance on the VAT control account at the date to which the return is prepared. This will be covered further later in your studies.

- **Balance c/d** – the closing balance on the account is usually carried down from the debit side, though if the business is due a refund of VAT from HMRC this amount will appear on the credit side.

- **Balance b/f** – the brought forward balance on the account at the beginning or end of the period is usually, but not always, a credit balance as most businesses record more output VAT (on sales) than input VAT (on purchases). A credit balance means that some money will have to be paid over at some stage to HMRC. A debit balance means that the business is due a refund of VAT by HMRC.

- **VAT on credit sales** – this is the VAT from the sales day book. It represents output VAT charged on sales which is payable to HMRC.

- **VAT on cash sales** – this is the VAT from the cash book (debit side). It represents output VAT charged on sales which is payable to HMRC.

- **VAT on purchases returns** – this is the VAT from the purchases returns day book.

- **VAT on the sale of assets owned for several years** – when an asset that has been owned for several years by the business, such as a machine, is sold, the sale is not recorded in the sales day book but in the journal (which we shall cover in Chapter 4). As a result the output VAT on the sale is recorded separately from output VAT on normal credit and cash sales.

- **VAT refunded by HMRC** – this is the amount that settles what HMRC owes to the business if input VAT exceeds output VAT.

The VAT control account must be accurately and promptly prepared, as VAT Returns and payments to HMRC must always be made on time in order to avoid penalties.

HOW IT WORKS

DP Printing has calculated that its output tax for May is £611.58 and its input tax for May is £395.70. It had a credit balance brought forward on its VAT account at 1 May of £250.00, which is paid on 14 May. The business's sales day book, purchases day book and cash book for the month of May are set out below (there are no returns day books), and we need to (a) prepare a VAT control account for May and (b) ensure that the final balance reconciles to the calculation prepared by the business.

Sales Day Book

Date	Customer	Total £	VAT £	Net £
3 May	J J Westrope	167.40	27.90	139.50
10 May	Virgo Partners	96.72	16.12	80.60
12 May	Jacks Ltd	107.64	17.94	89.70
15 May	J J Westrope	277.32	46.22	231.10
20 May	McGowan & Sons	595.08	99.18	495.90
23 May	Jacks Ltd	177.60	29.60	148.00
30 May	Virgo Partners	214.44	35.74	178.70
		1,636.20	272.70	1,363.50

Purchases Day Book

Date	Supplier	Total £	VAT £	Net £
5 May	Kilnfarm Paper	153.12	25.52	127.60
10 May	Jenkins Suppliers	219.96	36.66	183.30
12 May	Barnfield Ltd	317.16	52.86	264.30
20 May	Kilnfarm Paper	153.12	25.52	127.60
27 May	Jenkins Suppliers	451.32	75.22	376.10
30 May	Barnfield Ltd	312.24	52.04	260.20
		1,606.92	267.82	1,339.10

Cash Book – Debit Side

Date	Details	Discounts allowed £	Bank £	VAT £	Cash sales £	Trade receivables £
4 May	Cash sales		486.96	81.16	405.80	
4 May	Virgo Partners		117.38			117.38
10 May	Cash sales		451.80	75.30	376.50	
12 May	J J Westrope	8.73	308.86			308.86

Date	Details	Discounts allowed £	Bank £	VAT £	Cash sales £	Trade receivables £
15 May	McGowan & Sons		552.73			552.73
17 May	Cash sales		512.28	85.38	426.90	
20 May	Jacks Ltd		100.00			100.00
30 May	Cash sales		582.24	97.04	485.20	
		8.73	3,112.25	338.88	1,694.40	1,078.97

Cash Book – Credit Side

Date	Details	Discounts received £	Bank £	VAT £	Cash purchases £	Trade payables £	Sundry £
5 May	Cash purchases		230.52	38.42	192.10		
10 May	Jenkins Suppliers	17.67	423.89			423.89	
12 May	Kilnfarm Paper		150.00			150.00	
14 May	HMRC re VAT		250.00				250.00
15 May	Cash Purchases		321.84	53.64	268.20		
20 May	Barnfield Ltd	12.40	235.50			235.50	
27 May	Kilnfarm Paper		150.00			150.00	
30 May	Cash purchases		214.92	35.82	179.10		
		30.07	1,976.67	127.88	639.40	959.39	250.00

The VAT control account is prepared by:

- Entering the VAT column totals from all four day books provided

- Entering the amount paid to HMRC on 14 May in settlement of the opening credit balance due

- Carrying down a balance

VAT control account

	£		£
VAT on credit purchases	267.82	Balance b/f	250.00
VAT on cash purchases	127.88	VAT on credit sales	272.70
VAT paid to HMRC	250.00	VAT on cash sales	338.88
Balance c/d	215.88		
	861.58		861.58
		Balance b/f	215.88

CHAPTER OVERVIEW

- If all of the entries in the general ledger are correctly made then the totals of the closing balances on the sales and purchases ledgers should agree to the balances on the relevant control accounts

- The sales ledger control account will potentially have entries for dishonoured cheques and irrecoverable debts written off as well as the basic entries for invoices, credit notes, receipts from customers and discounts allowed

- The double entry for writing off an irrecoverable debt is to debit the irrecoverable debts expense account (NOT the sales account) and the VAT control account, and credit the sales ledger control account

- The purchases ledger control account will potentially have the basic entries for invoices, credit notes, payments made to suppliers and discounts received

- If all of the entries in the general ledger and subsidiary ledger have not been properly made, and/or if the lists of subsidiary ledger balances have been inaccurately prepared, then the subsidiary ledger balances totals will not agree to the balances on the control accounts – in which case the causes of the difference must be discovered

- A sales ledger control account reconciliation compares the balance on the sales ledger control account with the total of the trade receivables account balances in the sales ledger – both are amended for any errors that have been made, so the balance and the total should be the same after putting through the amendments

- An aged trade receivables analysis is used to monitor how slowly customers are paying their debts, and to make decisions about how/when to chase for payment

- A purchases ledger control account reconciliation works in exactly the same way as the sales ledger control account reconciliation, although all of the entries and balances are on the opposite sides

- The VAT control account potentially receives entries from all the books of prime entry, and is the means by which the business keeps track of what it owes HMRC (or what it is owed by HMRC)

Keywords

Aged trade receivables analysis – a schedule showing, for each trade receivable, how long the component parts of the balance have been unpaid

Irrecoverable debt – a debt which it is believed will never be recovered

Purchases ledger control account reconciliation – an exercise which agrees the balance on the purchases ledger control account to the total of the list of balances in the purchases ledger

Sales ledger control account reconciliation – an exercise which agrees the balance on the sales ledger control account to the total of the list of balances in the sales ledger

VAT control account – the account which shows how much VAT the business owes HMRC (credit balance) or is owed by HMRC (debit balance)

VAT return – a report to HMRC by registered businesses showing output less input VAT, and the amount of VAT owed to HMRC or refundable by HMRC

Writing off – removing an irrecoverable debt from the ledger accounts

TEST YOUR LEARNING

Test 1

Make entries in the sales ledger control account for the month of July from the following information:

	£
Opening balance 1 July	16,339
Credit sales for the month	50,926
Cash sales for the month	12,776
Sales returns (all for credit sales) for the month	3,446
Amount received from credit customers in the month	47,612
Settlement discounts allowed to credit customers in the month	1,658
Irrecoverable debt to be written off (total)	500
Customer cheque returned by the bank 'refer to drawer'	366

Sales ledger control account

	£		£

Test 2

Write up the purchases ledger control account for the month of July from the following information:

	£
Opening balance 1 July	12,587
Cash purchases for the month	15,600
Credit purchases for the month	40,827
Purchases returns (all for purchases on credit)	2,568
Cheques paid to trade payables in the month	38,227
Settlement discounts received from suppliers in the month	998

Purchases ledger control account

	£		£

BPP
LEARNING MEDIA

Test 3

The balance on a business's sales ledger control account at the end of June was £41,774 and the total of the list of trade receivable balances from the sales ledger came to £41,586.

The following errors were discovered:

(a) The sales day book was undercast by £100 on one page.

(b) A page from the sales returns day book with a total of £450 had not been posted to the control account, although the individual credit notes had been recorded in the sales ledger.

(c) An invoice from the sales day book had been posted to the individual account in the sales ledger as £769 instead of the correct figure of £679.

(d) A discount allowed to one customer of £16 had been posted to the wrong side of the customer's account in the sales ledger.

(e) An irrecoverable debt of £210 had been written off in the customer's individual account in the sales ledger but not in the general ledger.

(f) A credit balance in the sales ledger of £125 had been included in the list of balances as a debit balance.

Write up the sales ledger control account and reconcile to the total of the list of balances from the sales ledger after taking account of the errors noted.

Sales ledger control account

	£		£

BPP
LEARNING MEDIA

	£
Original total of list of balances	
Error 1	
Error 2	
Error 3	
Amended list of balances	
Amended control account balance	

Test 4

The balance on a business's purchases ledger control account at the end of June is £38,694 and the total of the list of balances in the purchases ledger came to £39,741.

The following errors were noted for the month:

(a)   A page in the purchases returns day book was overcast by £300.

(b)   A total from the cash book of £3,145 was posted in the general ledger as £3,415.

(c)   Settlement discounts received from suppliers of £267 were omitted from both the general ledger and the purchases ledger.

(d)   A credit note from a supplier for £210 was entered into the supplier's account in the purchases ledger as £120.

(e)   A debit balance on a supplier's account in the purchases ledger of £187 was omitted from the list of balances.

(f)   A credit balance in the purchases ledger should have been included in the list as £570 but instead was recorded as £770.

Write up the purchases ledger control account and reconcile to the total of the list of balances in the purchases ledger after taking account of these errors.

Purchases ledger control account

	£		£

	£
Original total of list of balances	
Error 1	
Error 2	
Error 3	
Error 4	
Amended list of balances	
Amended control account balance	

Test 5

This is a summary of transactions with suppliers during the month of August.

(a) Show whether each entry will be a debit or credit in the purchases ledger control account in the general ledger.

Details	Amount £	Debit ✓	Credit ✓
Amount due to credit suppliers at 1 August	42,394		
Payments to credit suppliers	39,876		
Purchases on credit	31,243		
Purchases returned to credit suppliers	1,266		
Discounts received	501		

(b) What will be the balance brought forward on 1 September on the above account?

	✓
Dr £31,994	
Cr £31,994	
Dr £34,526	
Cr £34,526	
Dr £32,996	
Cr £32,996	

(c) The following credit balances were in the purchases ledger on 1 September.

	£
Robinson Kate	8,239
Livesley Ltd	6,300
Townsend and Douglas	1,204
Miles Better Co	10,993
Strongarm Partners	4,375
Ambley Brothers	1,079

Reconcile the balances shown above with the purchases ledger control account balance you have calculated in part (b).

	£
Purchases ledger control account balance as at 31 August	
Total of purchases ledger accounts as at 31 August	
Difference	

(d) What may have caused the difference you calculated in part (c)?

	✓
A debit balance in the subsidiary ledger may have been included as a credit balance when calculating the total of the list of balances	
A credit balance in the subsidiary ledger may have been included as a debit balance when calculating the total of the list of balances	
A credit note may have been omitted from the purchases returns day book total	
Discounts received may only have been entered in the subsidiary ledger	

Test 6

The following is an extract from a business's books of prime entry.

Totals for three month period	
Sales day book	**Purchases day book**
Net: £145,360	Net: £71,840
VAT: £29,072	VAT: £14,368
Total: £174,432	Total: £86,208
Sales returns day book	**Purchases returns day book**
Net: £4,290	Net: £2,440
VAT: £858	VAT: £488
Total: £5,148	Total: £2,928
Cash book	
Net cash sales: £1,660	
VAT: £332	
Total cash sales: £1,992	

(a) Using the picklist of account names to complete the details columns, make the required entries in the VAT control account to record the VAT transactions in the period.

VAT control

Details	Amount £	Details	Amount £

Picklist of account names:

Cash book
Cash sales
Purchases
Purchases day book
Purchases returns

Sales
Sales day book
Sales returns
Sales returns day book

The VAT return has been completed and shows an amount owing from HM Revenue & Customs of £14,666.

(b)   Is the VAT return correct?

	✓
Yes	
No	

chapter 4:
THE JOURNAL

─────── **chapter coverage** 📖 ───────

In this chapter we introduce the final book of prime entry with which you are concerned: the journal. We see the format of a journal entry, and how the journal is used for making non-standard entries in the general and subsidiary ledgers, such as writing off irrecoverable debts. We also look at journal entries for entering opening balances in a new set of accounts, and for entering payroll transactions.

The topics covered are:

- ✍ The journal as a book of prime entry
- ✍ Preparing and posting a journal entry
- ✍ Uses of the journal
- ✍ Entering opening balances in a new set of accounts
- ✍ The journal and payroll transactions
- ✍ Voluntary deductions
- ✍ Gross pay to net pay
- ✍ Paying employees
- ✍ Accounting for payroll transactions
- ✍ Payments to HMRC and the pension scheme

THE JOURNAL AS A BOOK OF PRIME ENTRY

The cash book, the petty cash book and the sales and purchases day books contain transactions that are initially recorded from primary records. From these books of prime entry postings are made to the general ledger and the subsidiary sales and purchases ledgers.

The JOURNAL is the final book of prime entry that we need to look at. It is used to record transactions that do not appear in any of the other books of prime entry, so that they can then be posted to the ledgers. Often these are non-regular entries such as selling an asset that has been used in the business for some years, and writing off irrecoverable debts (both of these examples were covered in Chapter 3).

The journal consists of a series of JOURNAL ENTRIES. A single journal entry is a written instruction to the person maintaining the general ledger to make a double entry.

PREPARING AND POSTING A JOURNAL ENTRY

A typical journal entry that you would see in practice is given below:

Journal number:	0225		
Date:	5 April 20XX		
Authorised by:	D Fisher		
Account	*Reference*	*Debit* £	*Credit* £
Irrecoverable debts expense	GL023	700.00	
VAT control	GL009	140.00	
Sales ledger control	GL100		840.00
Total		840.00	840.00
R Sanderson	*SL072*		*840.00*
Narrative: Being the write-off of R Sanderson's debt			

The key points to be noted about the journal entry, intended to write off an irrecoverable debt, are:

- Each journal has a sequential number (0225 in this case) to ensure that all are entered into the ledger accounts.

- Each journal must be dated and authorised – the authorisation is vital as this is an adjustment to the ledger accounts.

- The general ledger accounts that are to be debited and credited are named and coded (GL023 etc).

- The amounts to be entered in each ledger account are set out, and whether they are to be debited or credited.

- A total is calculated for debits and for credits, to check that the amounts are the same and so the double entry is correct.

- If the entries also affect one of the subsidiary ledgers then the effect on it should also be set out, to ensure that it does not go out of line with the control accounts. This has been done in italic type here to make it clear that this part of the journal is not part of the general ledger double entry, and it includes the account name, the sales ledger/customer code, the amount and whether the entry is a debit or a credit.

- A narrative is included to describe what the journal entry is for.

In your assessment the style of journal entry that you will be required to prepare will not include a narrative. It will look like this:

Account name	Amount £	Debit ✓	Credit ✓

You choose the account name from a given picklist of names, you enter the figure in the 'amount' column, and then you place a tick in the debit or credit column as appropriate.

HOW IT WORKS

To prepare the journal for the irrecoverable debt write-off that we saw above, the following information is required:

- The names and ledger codes for the accounts affected (both in the general ledger and in the sales ledger)

- The amounts to be entered in each ledger account

- Whether each account needs to be debited or credited

- The authorisation for the transaction – all postings to the ledgers need to be authorised. Since most journal entries are non-standard it is particularly important that they are valid

Journal number:	0225		
Date:	5 April 20XX		
Authorised by:	D Fisher		
Account	*Reference*	*Debit* *£*	*Credit* *£*
Irrecoverable debts expense	GL023	700.00	
VAT control	GL009	140.00	
Sales ledger control	GL100		840.00
Total		840.00	840.00
R Sanderson	*SL072*		*840.00*
Narrative: Being the write-off of R Sanderson's debt			

In your assessment you would show this journal, as far as it affects the general ledger, as follows:

Account name	Amount £	Debit ✓	Credit ✓
Irrecoverable debts expense	700.00	✓	
VAT control	140.00	✓	
Sales ledger control	840.00		✓

In the assessment you may also need to prepare a journal for the sales ledger:

Account name	Amount £	Debit ✓	Credit ✓
R Sanderson	840.00		✓

The journal entries can now be posted to the four accounts that they affect:

General ledger

Sales ledger control   GL100

Date	Ref	Folio	£	Date	Ref	Folio	£
				5/4/XX	Irrecoverable debts expense	J0225	840.00

Irrecoverable debts expense   GL023

Date	Ref	Folio	£	Date	Ref	Folio	£
5/4/XX	Sales ledger control	J0225	700.00				

VAT control   GL009

Date	Ref	Folio	£	Date	Ref	Folio	£
5/4/XX	Sales ledger control	J0225	140.00				

Sales ledger

		R Sanderson					SL072
Date	Ref	Folio	£	Date	Ref	Folio	£
				5/4/XX	Irrecoverable debts expense	J022 5	840.00

Note that for each entry, the Ref column contains the name of the main account that takes the other side of the entry, and the Folio column contains the journal number. Since journal entries are non-standard it is particularly important that all this information is complete.

USES OF THE JOURNAL

Journal entries are most often used to correct errors, which we shall look at in Chapter 5, but you will also see them in your assessment in relation to:

- Writing off irrecoverable debts (see above)

- Recording the purchase or sale of major items used in the business over a period of time, known as NON-CURRENT ASSETS (see Chapter 3)

- Entering opening balances in a new set of ledger accounts

- Entering balances in the ledger accounts at the beginning of a new financial year

- Recording payroll transactions

ENTERING OPENING BALANCES IN A NEW SET OF ACCOUNTS

For a new business, or an existing business at the start of a new financial year, the journal is used to enter opening balances into its accounting system.

Entering opening asset and liability balances

It is a straightforward matter to enter the business's assets, liabilities and capital in the new set of accounts.

- Asset accounts are entered as debit balances.
- Liability and capital accounts are entered as credit balances.

Entering opening expense and income balances

Even before it has started its accounts a new business is likely to make some transactions. These will not only be to take out a loan, for instance, and pay the money into a business bank account (a liability and an asset, as we have just seen). It may also, for instance, pay rent in advance, get an inventory of stationery in, receive a down-payment from a credit customer, and have a phone line installed.

It is just as straightforward a matter to enter the business's expenses and income in the new set of accounts as it is to enter assets, liabilities and capital.

- Expenses accounts are debit balances.
- Income accounts are credit balances.

HOW IT WORKS

Sarah Clifford is starting a business on 1 November 20XX with the following balances:

	£
Bank loan	22,000
Capital	9,100
Cash at bank	6,550
Expenses	300
Non-current assets	25,000
Petty cash	450
Sales	1,200

We need to create a journal to enter the appropriate opening balances in Sarah's accounts as at 1 November 20XX.

Step 1   Draw up a journal entry to enter the opening balances in the new accounts. We just work through the list identifying balances as debits or credits.

Journal

Account name	Debit	Credit
	£	£
Bank loan		22,000
Capital		9,100
Cash at bank	6,550	
Expenses	300	
Non-current assets	25,000	
Petty cash	450	
Sales		1,200
Totals	32,300	32,300

96

Step 2 The second step is to enter the journal in the new set of accounts.

Bank loan account

			£				£
				1 Nov	Journal	22,000

Capital account

			£				£
				1 Nov	Journal	9,100

Cash at bank account

		£			£
1 Nov	Journal	6,550			

Expenses account

		£			£
1 Nov	Journal	300			

Non-current assets account

		£			£
1 Nov	Journal	25,000			

Petty cash account

		£			£
1 Nov	Journal	450			

Sales account

			£				£
				1 Nov	Journal	1,200

THE JOURNAL AND PAYROLL TRANSACTIONS

The entries in the accounting system that are made for payments to employees in respect of wages (or salaries) are known as PAYROLL TRANSACTIONS. To understand these you need to have a basic understanding of the way in which individuals are taxed in the UK.

Most employees receive an annual salary which is paid in regular intervals over the year, eg paid monthly. Some employees receive wages paid weekly. For our purposes salary and wages are the same so we will refer just to 'wages' from now on.

The amount that the employer owes the employee each month/week is known as their GROSS PAY.

Income tax and employee's NIC

An individual must pay INCOME TAX on all sources of income. The payment must be made to the UK tax collecting authority, HM Revenue & Customs (HMRC). The only tax on income that we are concerned about is the tax on wages that an employee earns, and we are not concerned with how the tax calculations are made.

Employees pay their income tax under the PAYE system, which stands for Pay-As-You Earn. This means that each time an employee is paid by their employer, the income tax for that month is deducted from their wages by the employer, and the employer then pays the income tax over to HMRC on the employee's behalf.

Employees must also pay employees' NATIONAL INSURANCE CONTRIBUTIONS (NIC) to HMRC. NIC are just another form of tax, calculated differently from income tax. An individual's employees' NIC are deducted from the employee's wages and paid over to HMRC together with the employee's income tax.

PAYE income tax and employees' NIC are known as STATUTORY DEDUCTIONS from gross pay, because the law (statute) requires employers to make these deductions.

There may be other (voluntary) deductions from gross pay as well. Once all deductions have been made, the amount paid to the employee is called NET PAY.

In the most simple of cases:

Gross pay – statutory deductions = net pay

HOW IT WORKS

Let's suppose that Ian is employed by Southfield. He earns £48,000 a year which is paid monthly. This means that each month his gross pay is (£48,000/12) = £4,000. Remember gross pay is the amount an employee earns before any deductions from pay.

The payroll department of Southfield has calculated that the income tax due by Ian for this month, October, is £770, and that his employees' NIC payment for the month should be £320.

Therefore, so far Ian's monthly net pay is calculated as follows:

	£	
Gross wages	4,000	
PAYE Income tax	(770)	Paid to HMRC by Southfield
NIC	(320)	Paid to HMRC by Southfield
Net pay	2,910	Paid to Ian by Southfield

This means that although Ian will receive a smaller amount each month than his gross pay he does not have to worry about paying any income tax or employees' NIC on his earnings to HMRC as it has already been done on his behalf by Southfield.

Employer's NIC

We have seen that at each pay day the employee must pay EMPLOYEES' NIC. The employer is also required to pay an additional amount of NIC for each employee, known as the EMPLOYER'S NIC. This is yet another form of tax, but the difference is that it is only suffered by the employer; there is no deduction from the employee's gross pay for employer's NIC. Employer's NIC is paid by the employer to HMRC.

HOW IT WORKS

When Southfield pay Ian each month they are also required to pay employer's NIC to HMRC.

Suppose that the employer's NIC for Ian is calculated as £415. In total, Southfield must pay HMRC in respect of Ian:

	£
PAYE deducted from gross pay	770
Employees' NIC deducted from gross pay	320
Employer's NIC suffered by Southfield	415
Total payable by Southfield to HMRC	1,505

VOLUNTARY DEDUCTIONS

There may also be other types of deduction from an employee's pay which are not required by the law but which have been chosen by the employee. These are VOLUNTARY DEDUCTIONS. The most common of these are pension contributions.

Pension contributions

Many employees pay a certain percentage of their gross pay into the business's pension scheme or into a scheme run by an external provider. PENSION CONTRIBUTIONS accumulate to provide a pension for the employee on their retirement. Like income tax and NIC, the employee's pension contribution is deducted from the employee's gross pay by the employer and paid into the pension scheme on the employee's behalf. Often the employer will itself also pay an amount into the pension scheme for that employee on each pay day, usually calculated as a percentage of the employee's gross pay. Like employer's NIC, the employer's pension contribution is not deducted from the employee's gross pay in arriving at net pay.

Give-as-you-earn scheme – GAYE

Employees can choose to pay money to an approved charity directly from their gross wages under the Give-As-You-Earn scheme, GAYE. The employee is allowed to pay any amount without limit per tax year and the employer deducts the money from the employee's gross pay and pays it over to the stated charity.

Other deductions

There are other deductions that can be made from an employee's gross pay, for example a regular subscription to the employee's trade union or the business's social club. If the employer makes a loan to an employee, say to help pay for an annual season ticket on public transport, regular repayments of this loan by the employee will be deducted by the employer in arriving at net pay.

GROSS PAY TO NET PAY

Once all of the statutory and voluntary deductions have been made from an employee's gross pay, what is left is the amount that the employee will actually receive – the net pay.

HOW IT WORKS

When Ian joined Southfield Electrical it was agreed that each month he would pay 5% of his gross pay into the company pension scheme, that is £200 per month. Southfield agree to make a further contribution to the pension scheme of 7.5% of Ian's gross pay.

We will now see all the elements of Ian's monthly pay and see who pays what to whom:

	£		
Gross pay	4,000.00		
PAYE Income tax	(770.00)	⟶	HMRC
Employees' NIC	(320.00)	⟶	HMRC
Pension contribution	(200.00)	⟶	Pension scheme
Net pay	2,710.00	⟶	Ian

So of the original gross wages of £4,000 per month Ian only receives £2,710. However the amount of income tax that he owed has been paid, as has the amount of NIC due from him, and he has also paid into his pension fund.

There are two further payments by Southfield to be made:

Employer's NIC	£415	⟶	HMRC
Employer's pension	£300	⟶	Pension scheme
(£4,000 × 7.5%)			

Task 1

Joan also works for Southfield and is paid on a weekly basis. Her gross pay is £400 per week. The payroll department has calculated that for this week the PAYE income tax payable is £69 and Joan's NIC for the week is £34. Joan also pays a weekly subscription of £2.50 to her trade union through the payroll.

What is Joan's net pay?

£

PAYING EMPLOYEES

Once the payroll department has made all of the calculations for each employee for that pay day then the employees must be actually paid.

Methods of payment

Cash

It is possible to pay employees in cash. However, the practical and security arrangements required mean that this is now rarely done.

Cheque

It is also possible to pay each employee's net pay with a cheque. Again, however, this is a time-consuming process as a cheque must be written out for each

individual's net pay. Payment by this method would normally only be in an organisation with a small number of employees or for one-off payments for work carried out.

BACS

The most common method of making payroll payments is automated payment (direct credit) by BACS, Bankers Automated Clearing System. This ensures that the net pay for each employee is paid directly into that employee's bank account. The total payment for all employees is taken from the business's bank account by its bank.

ACCOUNTING FOR PAYROLL TRANSACTIONS

The entries into the general ledger accounts for the payroll transactions may seem fairly complex but if you bear in mind the system that has just been considered they can be followed through logically:

- The full cost of employing an employee is:

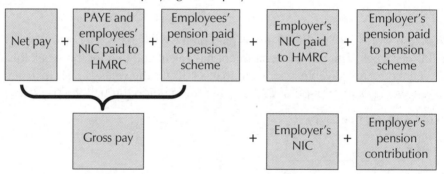

Therefore gross pay plus employer's NIC plus employer's pension contribution is the cost of employing employees and must be what appears as the wages expense for the business.

- The PAYE and NIC that is deducted from the employees' gross pay plus the employer's NIC must normally be paid over to HMRC by the 19th of the month following pay day. Therefore these amounts are payables until they are paid and must appear in a liability account. The total is not normally classified as a 'trade payable' since the entity to which money is owed is HMRC, not a supplier with which the business trades. Sometimes instead it is referred to as an 'other payable'.

- The pension contribution that is deducted from the employee's gross pay plus the employer's pension contribution must be paid over to the pension scheme. Again, the total is an 'other payable' until it is paid and must appear in a liability account.

BPP LEARNING MEDIA

The double entry reflects these factors and uses four main accounts:

- The WAGES CONTROL ACCOUNT
- The wages expense account
- The HMRC account
- The pension payable account

(There may be other payable accounts if further voluntary deductions are made, say in respect of GAYE, trade union and social club subscriptions. If there is an employee loan outstanding, the repayments deducted in arriving at net pay are entered in the loan account, which is an asset account, since the employee is the business's receivable.)

There are a number of double entries to be made:

- Gross pay:

    - **Debit** entry in the wages expense account
    - **Credit** entry in the wages control account

- Net pay paid to employees:

    - **Debit** entry in the wages control account
    - **Credit** entry in the cash book (credit side)

- PAYE and employees' NIC deducted from gross pay

    - **Debit** entry in the wages control account
    - **Credit** entry in the HMRC account

- Employees' pension contributions deducted from gross pay

    - **Debit** entry in the wages control account
    - **Credit** entry in the pension payable account

- Employer's NIC

    - **Debit** entry in the wages expense account
    - **Credit** entry in the wages control account

    and

    - **Debit** entry in the wages control account
    - **Credit** entry in the HMRC account

- Employer's pension contributions

    - **Debit** entry in the wages expense account
    - **Credit** entry in the wages control account

    and

    - **Debit** entry in the wages control account
    - **Credit** entry in the pension payable account

HOW IT WORKS

We return to Ian's wages payment which is summarised below:

	£
Gross wages	4,000
PAYE Income tax	(770)
Employees' NIC	(320)
Employee's pension contribution	(200)
Net pay	2,710
Employer's NIC	415
Employer's pension contribution	300

The entries in the ledger accounts would be as follows:

- Gross pay of £4,000 added to wages expense

Wages expense account

	£		£
Wages control	4,000		

Wages control account

	£		£
		Wages expense	4,000

- Net pay of £2,710 paid to employee from the bank account

Wages control account

	£		£
Bank	2,710	Wages expense	4,000

Bank account

	£		£
		Wages control	2,710

- PAYE income tax of £770 and employee's NIC of £320 deducted from gross pay

Wages control account

	£		£
Bank	2,710	Wages expense	4,000
HMRC (770 + 320)	1,090		

HMRC account

	£		£
		Wages control	1,090

- Employee's pension contribution of £200 deducted from gross pay

Wages control account

	£		£
Bank	2,710	Wages expense	4,000
HMRC	1,090		
Pension payable	200		

Pension payable account

	£		£
		Wages control	200

- Employer's NIC of £415 added to wages expense

Wages control account

	£		£
Bank	2,710	Wages expense	4,000
HMRC	1,090	Wages expense	415
Pension payable	200		
HMRC	415		

Wages expense account

	£		£
Wages control	4,000		
Wages control	415		

HMRC

	£		£
		Wages control	1,090
		Wages control	415

- Employer's pension contribution of £300 added to wages expense

Wages control account

	£		£
Bank	2,710	Wages expense	4,000
HMRC	1,090	Wages expense	415
Pension payable	200	Wages expense	300
HMRC	415		
Pension payable	300		
	4,715		4,715

Wages expense account

	£		£
Wages control	4,000		
Wages control	415		
Wages control	300		

Pension payable account

£			£
		Wages control	200
		Wages control	300

Summary of double entry

- The wages control account is a clearing account which helps to ensure that the double entry is made correctly. If so, the account should balance to zero at the end of each period (see above).

- The wages expense account shows the cost of employing Ian, ie gross pay plus employer's NIC plus employer's pension contribution.

- The HMRC account shows how much must be paid over to HM Revenue & Customs by the 19th of the following month.

- The pension payable account shows how much should be paid into the pension scheme.

Task 2

Joan works for Southfield and is paid on a weekly basis. Her gross pay is £400 per week. Her PAYE income tax is £69 for the week and her NIC for the week is £33. Joan also pays a weekly subscription to her trade union through the payroll of £2.50. Southfield's NIC contribution for Joan for this week is £41. What are the balances on the following accounts (before any payments are made to HMRC)?

The HMRC account

£	

The wages expense account

£	

The payroll and the payroll journal entry

In practice, the double entry considered above would not be made for each individual employee. Instead the details of gross pay, statutory and voluntary deductions, net pay, employer's NIC and pension for each employee would be recorded in what is known as a 'payroll'. From this primary record a payroll journal entry would be prepared on each pay day, summarising the required double entry. It is the journal, therefore, that is the book of prime entry for recording payroll transactions. The summary journal for Southfield's payroll (in relation to Ian) would be as follows:

Journal

Account name	Debit £	Credit £
Wages expense	4,715	
Pension payable		500
HMRC		1,505
Bank		2,710
Totals	4,715	4,715

Alternatively, the business could prepare a more detailed journal that contained all the double entry involving the wages control account that we followed through earlier.

PAYMENTS TO HMRC AND THE PENSION SCHEME

The PAYE and NIC deducted from the employees' gross pay and the employer's NIC must be paid over to HMRC each month by the employer. The payment must normally be made within 14 days of the tax month end, which is the 5th of each month. So payment must reach HMRC by the 19th of each month. Similarly, the contributions to the pension scheme must be paid over in line with the relevant agreement.

When the payments are made, the relevant payable account is debited and the bank account is credited.

CHAPTER OVERVIEW

- The journal is the book of prime entry for all non-standard transactions to be recorded in the accounting system, including the recording of:

    – Opening balances for assets, liabilities and capital at the beginning of a new business

    – Payroll transactions

- In the UK individuals pay income tax on all of their income at various rates depending upon the amount of that income

- If a person is employed then they will pay their income tax through the PAYE system

- A further statutory deduction from the employee's gross pay is employees' National Insurance Contributions (NIC)

- The employer must also pay employer's NIC for each employee who earns more than a stated amount per week

- The PAYE deducted, the employees' NIC deducted and the employer's NIC will all be paid over to HMRC by the employer

- There are also other, non-statutory amounts that may be deducted from an employee's gross pay – pension contributions, GAYE payments, trade union and social club subscriptions, loan repayments etc

- Wages may be paid in cash or by cheque but the most common method is by BACS

- The ledger entries for payroll transactions take place in three main general ledger accounts – the wages control account, the wages expense account and the HMRC account

- In practice, the journal is used as the book of prime entry for the summary figures from the payroll in which details of gross pay, deductions and net pay will be recorded for each employee each month

- The PAYE and NIC due must be paid to HMRC normally by the 19th of the month following the pay day

Keywords

Gross pay – the salary/wage payable to an employee before any statutory or voluntary deductions

HMRC – HM Revenue & Customs, the UK government department responsible for collecting tax

Income tax – a tax that is paid by individuals on all sources of income, including salaries and wages

Journal – the book of prime entry that is used to record transactions that do not appear in any of the other books of prime entry

Journal entry – a written instruction to the bookkeeper to make a double entry into the general and/or subsidiary ledgers

National Insurance Contributions (employer's NIC) – an additional tax, suffered by the employer, based on an employee's gross pay

National Insurance Contributions (employees' NIC) – a tax on employees' income

Net pay – the amount of the employee's wages actually paid to the employee, net of statutory and voluntary deductions

Non-current asset – a large item, such as a building, vehicle or machine, which is used by the business over several years

PAYE system – the system which allows the employer to pay employees their salaries net of income tax (and NICs), and to pay it to HMRC on the employees' behalf

Payroll transactions – payments to employees in respect of salaries and wages

Pension contribution – a form of voluntary deduction from employees, and a contribution from employers in addition, which builds up in the hands of the pension administrator to provide a pension for the employee on retirement

Statutory deductions – deductions made by the employer from an employee's pay in respect of income tax and employees' NIC

Voluntary deductions – non-statutory amounts deducted from employees' pay with their consent eg Give-As-You-Earn (GAYE) and trade union subscriptions

Wages control account – a clearing account used to ensure that the double entry for payroll transactions is correct

TEST YOUR LEARNING

Test 1

Prepare a journal entry for recording the following opening balances in a new set of accounts: capital £7,500, trade receivables £2,000, trade payables £2,500, cash at bank £8,000.

Account name	Amount £	Debit ✓	Credit ✓

Test 2

State whether the following deductions from gross pay are statutory or voluntary deductions:

	Statutory deduction ✓	Voluntary deduction ✓
Pension contributions		
Income tax		
Employee's NIC		
Trade union fees		

Test 3

An employee earns a gross salary of £27,000 per year and is paid on a monthly basis. For the month of October the payroll department has calculated a PAYE income tax deduction of £418.16 and NI contributions due of £189.00 from the employee and £274.50 from the employer.

(a) What is the employee's net pay?

£

(b) Record the payroll transactions for this employee in the ledger accounts.

Wages control account

	£		£

Wages expense account

	£		£

HMRC account

	£		£

Bank account

	£		£

Test 4

One of Grangemouth Ltd's credit customers, Markham Co, has ceased trading, owing Grangemouth Ltd £1,290 plus VAT.

(a) Using the picklist of account names, record the journal entries needed in the general ledger to write off the net amount and the VAT.

Account name	Amount £	Debit ✓	Credit ✓

Picklist of account names:

Irrecoverable debts
Grangemouth Ltd
Markham Co
Purchases
Purchases ledger control
Sales
Sales ledger control
VAT

(b) A new business, Carswell & Sons, is opening a new set of accounts. A partially completed journal to record the opening entries is shown below.

Record the journal entries needed in the accounts in the general ledger of Carswell & Sons to deal with the opening entries.

Account name	Amount £	Debit ✓	Credit ✓
Capital	18,410		
Cash at bank	3,270		
Heat and light	300		
Loan from bank	5,000		
Machinery	10,000		
Motor vehicle	7,800		
Petty cash	200		
Rent paid	1,300		
Stationery	190		
Vehicle expenses	350		
Journal to record the opening entries of new business			

Test 5

A business pays its employees by BACS every month and maintains a wages control account. A summary of last month's payroll transactions is shown below:

Item	£
Gross wages	12,756
Employer's NIC	1,020
Employees' NIC	765
Income tax	1,913
Loan repayment	100

Using the picklist of account names, record the journal entries needed in the general ledger to:

(a) Record the wages expense

Account name	Amount £	Debit ✓	Credit ✓

(b) Record the amount payable to HMRC

Account name	Amount £	Debit ✓	Credit ✓

(c) Record the net wages paid to the employees

Account name	Amount £	Debit ✓	Credit ✓

(d) Record the loan repayment

Account name	Amount £	Debit ✓	Credit ✓

Picklist of account names:

Bank
Employees' NIC
Employer's NIC
HM Revenue & Customs
Income tax
Net wages
Loan
Wages control
Wages expense

chapter 5:
ERRORS AND THE TRIAL BALANCE

chapter coverage 📖

This chapter considers a trial balance that does not balance, which indicates that the double entry has not operated properly so there are errors in the general ledger accounts. You are expected to identify errors, correct them using a suspense account and the journal, and then re-draft the trial balance. In order to identify the errors you need to be aware of the different types of error that exist, both those that are shown up by the trial balance and those that are not. The topics covered are:

✎ Types of error

✎ Imbalance on the trial balance

✎ Correcting an error that does not cause an imbalance

✎ Correcting an error that does cause an imbalance – using the suspense account

✎ Correcting errors

✎ Redrafting the trial balance

TYPES OF ERROR

In any accounting system there are several types of error that can be made when making entries in the ledger accounts. Some of these errors will be identified when a trial balance is extracted but there are a number of types of error that can take place yet the trial balance will still balance.

You must be able to identify both the type of error and its effect on whether the trial balance will still balance.

Transposition errors

Before we look at types of error, we will consider a particular slip which frequently occurs, and which can be, but is not necessarily, the source of imbalances in the trial balance: transposition errors. A TRANSPOSITION ERROR is where the digits in a number are transposed (swapped round), for example:

- A transaction for £435 is recorded correctly as a debit entry in one general ledger account, but the credit entry is made at £345 (3 and 4 swapped).

- The balance on a general ledger account is transposed when it is taken to the trial balance, eg a debit balance of £1,268 is recorded in the trial balance as a debit balance of £1,628 (2 and 6 swapped).

- A payment of £520 from a credit customer is recorded in the cash book as £250 (2 and 5 swapped).

The first two errors mean that the trial balance does not balance, as debits and credits are not equal. The third example will NOT cause an imbalance in the debits and credits in the trial balance, since the transposition error arose in the book of prime entry: the same incorrect amount is the debit entry in the cash book and the credit entry in the sales ledger control account.

If a transposition error has been made that affects the trial balance – and it is the only error – then the difference between the total debits and the total credits in the trial balance will be exactly divisible by 9. This is a very useful trick to know when trying to track down errors.

Errors leading to an imbalance on the trial balance

Several types of error will mean that the debit balances on the trial balance will not equal the credit balances.

Single entry errors – only one side of the double entry has been made in the general ledger accounts, eg the debit and not the credit.

Unequal amounts error – one side of the double entry is made accurately but an error is made in the other side, for example a transaction for £435 is recorded correctly as a debit entry in one general ledger account, but a transposition error is made in recording the credit entry at £345, so the debit and credit entries are not equal.

Two debits/two credits error – instead of entering a transaction as a debit in one account and a credit in another, a common error is to make debit entries in both accounts, or credit entries in both accounts. This means that one account will be correct but the other will be out of balance by twice the amount of the entry. For instance, to record discounts received of £500, the correct entry is to debit Purchases ledger control with £500 and credit Discounts received with £500, so there is a debit balance of £500 on PLCA and a credit balance of £500 on Discounts received. If instead a credit entry is made in each account, both have credit balances of £500. To bring the PLCA to the correct balance we have to debit it with £500 to correct the error, and then debit it again to make the correct entry:

Purchases ledger control account

	£		£
Correct incorrect entry	500	Incorrect entry	500
Make correct entry	500	Balance c/d	500
	1,000		1,000
Balance b/f	500		

Calculation error – a mistake is made in calculating the balance on a ledger account so an incorrect balance is included in the trial balance.

Balance transfer error – a balance on a general ledger account is transferred incorrectly into the trial balance. This error can occur in two ways: a debit balance of say £760 could be transferred to the trial balance as a debit balance of £670 (so a transposition error is the source of a balance transfer error), or the debit balance of £760 could be transferred to the trial balance as a credit balance of £760.

Balance omission – a balance on a general ledger account is omitted from the trial balance.

Task 1

A sales invoice recorded in the sales day book for a sale of £1,678 plus VAT has been correctly recorded in the sales ledger control account and VAT account but has been entered into the sales account as £1,768. This is a:

Single entry error

Transposition error

Calculation error

Balance omission error

which | will / will not | cause an imbalance in the trial balance.

Errors which do not cause an imbalance on the trial balance

There are several types of error that do not cause an imbalance on the trial balance and therefore do not show up through the trial balance process – though they must still be found of course!

Error of original entry – here both entries into the general ledger, debit and credit, are made using the wrong amount. This may be because:

- The transaction was recorded in the primary record or the book of prime entry at the incorrect amount, or

- The wrong figure was picked up from the primary record (eg a transposition error was made) and this incorrect figure was used for both the debit and the credit entry in the general ledger.

Error of omission – an entry is completely omitted from the general ledger accounts.

Error of reversal of entries – the correct figure has been used and a debit and a credit entry made but the debit and the credit are on the wrong sides of the respective accounts.

Error of commission – the double entry is arithmetically correct but a wrong account of the **same type** has been used. For example, if the phone bill is paid the bank account is credited and an expense account, the phone account, should be debited. If, instead, the electricity account is debited this is an error of commission. It does not affect the trial balance but it does mean that both the phone account and electricity account show the wrong balance.

Error of principle – this is similar to an error of commission in that the double entry is arithmetically correct but the **wrong type** of account is used. For example, if printer cartridges are purchased, the bank account is credited and the computer expenses or office expenses account should be debited. If, instead, the cost of the cartridges is debited to a non-current asset account (ie it is treated as capital expenditure rather than revenue expenditure), this is an error of principle.

Compensating errors – these are probably rare in practice but it is where two errors are made which exactly cancel each other out. For example, if the sales ledger control account is debited with £100 too much in respect of a sales transaction and the purchases returns account is credited with £100 too much in respect of a purchases returns transaction, the two errors cancel each other out. The errors are unrelated but the fact that they both occurred will mean that there is no imbalance in the trial balance to help identify them.

Task 2

What type of error is each of the following?

A transaction for £435 is recorded correctly as a debit entry in one general ledger account, but the credit entry is made at £345.

☐ Error of original entry

☐ Balance transfer error

☐ Unequal amounts error

A general ledger account debit balance of £1,268 is recorded in the trial balance as a debit balance of £1,628.

☐ Error of original entry

☐ Balance transfer error

☐ Unequal amounts error

A payment of £520 from a credit customer is recorded in the cash book as £250.

☐ Error of original entry

☐ Balance transfer error

☐ Unequal amounts error

Task 3

A sales invoice to J K Reynolds was recorded in the sales ledger in the account of T M Reynolds. This is (please tick)

An error of original entry

An error of principle

A commission error

An omission error

IMBALANCE ON THE TRIAL BALANCE

If the trial balance does not balance then the reason or reasons for this must be discovered. As we have seen, there are several types of error that could cause the total of the debits not to equal the total of the credits in the general ledger. Rather than going back to each ledger account and checking each entry to find the cause of the imbalance it makes sense in practice to take a logical approach to finding the causes of any imbalance.

The problem might be arithmetical or it may be to do with the double entry, but it makes sense to check the more obvious and simpler errors before getting involved with detailed checking of the ledger accounts.

Procedure for finding the error/errors

Step 1   Check the totalling of the debit column and the credit column on the trial balance. It is very easy to make an error when totalling a long column of figures so this is an obvious place to start.

Step 2   Calculate the difference between the debit and credit total – this may come in useful later in the checking exercise if the difference cannot be found easily (see Steps 6 and 7).

Step 3   Check that the amount of each balance in the general ledger has been correctly copied into the trial balance and that each has been included on the correct side, debit or credit.

Step 4   Check that all the balances in the general ledger have been included in the trial balance. In particular, ensure that the cash and bank balances and the petty cash balances have been included as these are generally kept physically separate from the general ledger since the cash book and petty cash book are usually both books of prime entry and part of the general ledger.

Step 5   Check the calculation of the balance on each ledger account is correct.

Step 6   Look in the ledger accounts for any entry that is for the same amount as the difference on the trial balance. If this amount is found, check that the double entry for the relevant transaction has been correctly carried out.

Step 7   Look in the ledger accounts for any entry that is for half the amount of the difference on the trial balance. If this is found, check that the double entry for the relevant transaction has been correctly carried out.

If all else fails you have to:

Step 8   Check all the bookkeeping entries from the books of prime entry since the date of the last trial balance, and then

Step 9   Check that all the books of prime entry have been written up from primary documents and totalled correctly.

Number tricks to look out for

We have already seen that if the difference on the trial balance is divisible exactly by 9 then if there is a single error it is likely to be one of transposition. This means that two digits in a figure have been reversed, eg £654 is entered as £564 – the difference of £90 is exactly divisible by 9.

If the difference on the trial balance is a round number, eg £10, £100, £1,000 etc then if there is a single error it is likely to be an arithmetical one. Therefore take great care when checking account balance calculations and the transfer of balances into the trial balance.

CORRECTING AN ERROR THAT DOES NOT CAUSE AN IMBALANCE

Each error or omission must be corrected and this is done using a journal entry. We shall concentrate first on errors that do not cause an imbalance on the trial balance.

HOW IT WORKS

In a business which does not charge VAT on sales, the sales day book for a period is £1,000 less than it should be (it has been undercast by £1,000). This means that both the sales ledger control account and the sales account are £1,000 too small (they have been understated by £1,000). This error was probably picked up

when the SLCA did not reconcile with the total of the sales ledger balances. Because the postings to the individual sales ledger accounts are of the individual invoice totals, they are unaffected by the calculation of a wrong overall total in the sales day book, whereas the two general ledger accounts will both be entered with the incorrect total.

Both general ledger accounts must have an additional entry. This is done by writing out a journal to make the right entries. As there is only one debit amount and one credit amount we do not need to calculate a total to double check that the general ledger postings will be correct.

Date	Ref	Debit	Credit
20XX			
		£	£
Sales ledger control account	GL94	1,000	
Sales account	GL02		1,000
Being correction of the undercasting of the sales day book			

CORRECTING AN ERROR THAT DOES CAUSE AN IMBALANCE – USING THE SUSPENSE ACCOUNT

If the debit total does not equal the credit total when the trial balance is initially drafted then the reasons for this must be investigated and eventually corrected. Until the reasons for the imbalance on the trial balance have been discovered and corrected a SUSPENSE ACCOUNT is opened in order to make the trial balance totals equal.

HOW IT WORKS

A business drafted its initial trial balance and found the totals of the debit and credit columns were as follows:

	Debit £	Credit £
Total	157,600	157,900

The difference of £300 is initially dealt with by opening a suspense account in order to create a balanced trial balance.

	Debit £	Credit £
Original total balances	157,600	157,900
Suspense account	300	
Trial balance totals	157,900	157,900

The trial balance now balances but there is also a temporary new general ledger account, the suspense account, with a debit balance.

Suspense account

	£		£
Balance b/f	300		

This balance must **not** remain in the ledger accounts. The reasons for the imbalance on the trial balance must be investigated and corrections must be made using journal entries. Once the corrections have been put through the suspense account will be cleared to a balance of zero.

CORRECTING ERRORS

In an assessment you will need to identify the errors that have occurred from information given to you, and then draft the journal entries to correct them. The procedure to follow is:

- Identify what the incorrect double entry was, then
- Determine what the correct double entry should have been, then
- Prepare the journal entries:
    - Reverse the incorrect double entry, and
    - Make the correct double entry.

(Note that it is also possible in practice to make net journal entries, which reverse and correct only the incorrect original entries, leaving the parts of the entries that were made correctly the first time unaffected. In the AAT assessment, however, you need to follow the 'reverse and correct' approach, as we shall see from now on.)

Not all errors affect the balancing of the trial balance so when you draft journals to correct errors you will not always have to make an entry in the suspense account.

The only time there will be a suspense account entry in the journal is when the original double entry broke down in some way. This means there will be one reversing double entry in a normal general ledger account and the suspense account, followed by a correcting double entry in the normal general ledger accounts.

HOW IT WORKS

Continuing with the previous example where there is a debit balance of £300 on the suspense account, you are now told that the business does not account for VAT and the following errors have been discovered:

(1) Discounts received of £175 have been omitted from the general ledger accounts.

(2) Sales returns were correctly recorded as £1,500 in the sales returns account but as only £1,000 in the sales ledger control account.

(3) When the rent paid account was balanced it was undercast by £1,000.

(4) A purchase invoice for £460 was omitted from the Purchases Day Book.

(5) Purchases returns of £580 were recorded in the general ledger as £850.

(6) Discounts allowed of £200 were only entered in the discounts allowed account.

(7) A receipt from a credit customer of £140 was entered on the wrong side of the trade receivable's account in the sales ledger.

We will deal with each of these errors in turn.

(1) Discounts received of £175 have been omitted from the general ledger accounts

This has been omitted from the general ledger totally (error of omission) so there is no need for a reversing double entry. We just need to make the full double entry for discounts received.

Account name	Amount £	Debit	Credit
Purchases ledger control	175	✓	
Discounts received	175		✓

(2) Sales returns were correctly recorded as £1,500 in the sales returns account but as only £1,000 in the sales ledger control account

First of all we must identify the original incorrect double entry for this unequal amounts error. The sales returns account was debited with £1,500 and the SLCA was credited with £1,000. Where was the other £500 credited? While the entry was not physically made, in effect £500 was credited to the suspense account. These incorrect entries must therefore be reversed, and then the correct entries can be made.

Account name	Amount £	Debit	Credit
Reversing entries:			
Sales returns	1,500		✓
Sales ledger control	1,000	✓	
Suspense	500	✓	
Correcting entries:			
Sales returns	1,500	✓	
Sales ledger control	1,500		✓

The effect on the suspense account is as follows:

Suspense account

	£		£
Balance b/f	300		
Sales returns	500		

(3) **When the rent paid account was balanced it was undercast by £1,000**

As a result of this calculation error the rent balance in the trial balance has to be increased by £1,000, but this is the only entry required so the other side of the entry must be to the suspense account.

Account name	Amount £	Debit	Credit
Rent	1,000	✓	
Suspense	1,000		✓

The effect on the suspense account is as follows:

Suspense account

	£		£
Balance b/f	300	Rent	1,000
Sales returns	500		

(4) **A purchase invoice for £460 was omitted from the purchases day book**

This is an error of omission: the invoice was not entered in the purchases day book so it has not been entered in the general ledger. Therefore the full double entry is required.

Account name	Amount £	Debit	Credit
Purchases	460	✓	
Purchases ledger control	460		✓

(5) Purchases returns of £580 were recorded in the general ledger as £850

In this error of original entry both sides of the entry for purchases returns are too high by £270 which, as it is divisible by 9, suggests that a transposition error was made. The original double entry must be reversed and the correct double entry made.

Account name	Amount £	Debit	Credit
Reversing entries:			
Purchases ledger control	850		✓
Purchases returns	850	✓	
Correcting entries:			
Purchases ledger control	580	✓	
Purchases returns	580		✓

(6) Discounts allowed of £200 were only entered in the discounts allowed account

In this single entry error the discount was only entered in the discounts allowed account, so the missing credit entry was effectively made to the suspense account when it should have been made to the sales ledger control account. We must reverse the original incorrect double entry then make the correct ones.

Account name	Amount £	Debit	Credit
Reversing entries:			
Discounts allowed	200		✓
Suspense	200	✓	
Correcting entries:			
Discounts allowed	200	✓	
Sales ledger control	200		✓

The effect on the suspense account is as follows:

Suspense account

	£		£
Balance b/f	300	Rent	1,000
Sales returns	500		
Discounts allowed	200		

(7) **A receipt from a credit customer of £140 was entered on the wrong side of the trade receivable's account in the sales ledger**

As this reversal of entry error was made in the sales ledger it does not affect the double entry so there is no requirement for any alteration to the general ledger accounts, though the sales ledger should of course be corrected, otherwise the totals of the balances will not agree with the balance on the sales ledger control account.

Clearing the suspense account

Once all of the errors have been dealt with via journal entries, there should be no remaining balance on the suspense account.

Suspense account

	£		£
Balance b/f	300	Rent	1,000
Sales returns	500		
Discount allowed	200		
	1,000		1,000

Task 4

A receipt from a credit customer of £1,250 was entered on the debit side in both the cash book and the sales ledger control account.

What are the journal entries required to reverse the original entries and make the correct ones in the ledger accounts?

Account name	Amount £	Debit ✓	Credit ✓
Reversing entries:			
Correcting entries:			

REDRAFTING THE TRIAL BALANCE

Once the suspense account has been opened and cleared the trial balance can be redrafted.

HOW IT WORKS

Harry Naylor runs a small business and does not charge VAT on his sales. He has handed you the following balances on his ledger accounts that he has prepared.

Cash book

	Cash £	Bank £		Cash £	Bank £
Bal b/f	1,000	2,390			

Capital account

	£		£
		Bal b/f	10,000

Non-current assets account

	£		£
Bal b/f	20,000		

BPP LEARNING MEDIA

Purchases account

	£		£
Bal b/f	13,100		

Purchases ledger control account

	£		£
		Bal b/f	550

Rent account

	£		£
Bal b/f	600		

Sales account

	£		£
		Bal b/f	33,291

Sales ledger control account

	£		£
Bal b/f	5,925		

Petty cash

	£		£
Bal b/f	135		

Stationery account

	£		£
Bal b/f	200		

Drawings account

	£		£
Bal b/f	500		

Discounts allowed

	£		£
Bal b/f	50		

Discounts received

	£		£
		Bal b/f	100

Harry is aware that he has made two mistakes as follows:

(a) He entered one sales day book total correctly as £1,298 in the sales ledger control account but as £1,289 in the sales account (an unequal amounts error).

(b) He omitted the posting to the purchases ledger control account when recording discounts received of £50 (a single entry error).

These are the steps to follow:

- Draw up an initial trial balance, calculating and inserting a suspense account balance if this is needed to make it balance.

Account name	Debit £	Credit £
Cash in hand	1,000	
Cash at bank	2,390	
Capital		10,000
Non-current assets	20,000	
Purchases	13,100	
PLCA		550
Rent	600	
Sales		33,291
SLCA	5,925	
Petty cash	135	
Stationery	200	
Drawings	500	
Discounts allowed	50	
Discounts received		100
Suspense	41	
Totals	43,941	43,941

- Open up the suspense ledger account.

Suspense account

	£		£
Bal b/f	41		

- Prepare journal entries to make the necessary corrections to the ledger accounts.

(a) The original entry should have been debit SLCA £1,298 and credit sales £1,298. Too little (£1,298 – £1,289 = £9) was credited to sales, so as this creates an imbalance on the trial balance we know that effectively £9 was credited to the suspense account. We need to reverse the original entries and make the correct ones:

Account name	Amount £	Debit	Credit
Reversing entries:			
Sales account	1,289	✓	
Suspense account	9	✓	
SLCA	1,298		✓
Correcting entries:			
SLCA	1,298	✓	
Sales	1,298		✓

(b) The original entry should have been debit PLCA £50 and credit discounts received £50. The PLCA posting was omitted entirely, so effectively £50 was debited to the suspense account. We need to reverse the original entries and make the correct ones.

Account name	Amount £	Debit	Credit
Reversing entries:			
Discounts received	50	✓	
Suspense account	50		✓
Correcting entries:			
PLCA	50	✓	
Discounts received	50		✓

- Process the journal entries in the ledger accounts and balance them.

Sales account

	£		£
SLCA	1,289	Bal b/f	33,291
Bal c/d	33,300	SLCA	1,298
	34,589		34,589
		Bal b/f	33,300

Sales ledger control account

	£		£
Bal b/f	5,925	Sales/suspense	1,298
Sales	1,298	Bal c/d	5,925
	7,223		7,223
Bal b/f	5,925		

Discounts received

	£		£
Suspense	50	Bal b/f	100
Bal c/d	100	PLCA	50
	150		150
		Bal b/f	100

Purchases ledger control account

	£		£
Discounts received	50	Bal b/f	550
Bal c/d	500		
	550		550
		Bal b/f	500

Suspense account

	£		£
Bal b/f	41	Discounts received	50
SLCA	9		
	50		50

- Redraft the trial balance.

Account name	Debit £	Credit £
Cash in hand	1,000	
Cash at bank	2,390	
Capital		10,000
Non-current assets	20,000	
Purchases	13,100	
PLCA		500
Rent	600	
Sales		33,300
SLCA	5,925	
Petty cash	135	
Stationery	200	
Drawings	500	
Discounts allowed	50	
Discounts received		100
~~Suspense~~	~~41~~	–
Revised totals	**43,900**	**43,900**

CHAPTER OVERVIEW

- Some errors in the accounting records cause an imbalance on the trial balance – these include single entry rather than double entry, debit and credit entries of unequal amounts, entries of two debits or two credits, a calculation error, a balance transfer error and a balance being omitted from the trial balance

- Errors in the accounting records which do not cause an imbalance on the trial balance are errors of original entry, errors of omission, errors of reversal of entries, errors of commission, errors of principle and compensating errors

- Finding the error or errors when total debits do not agree with total credits on the trial balance involves carrying out basic arithmetical checks before examining the detailed double entry and the initial recording in the books of prime entry

- If the trial balance does not balance, set up a suspense account to make the debits equal to the credits

- Once the errors have been found, for each one:

  - Work out what the original, incorrect double entry was (including effective entries in the suspense account) and what the correct double entry should be

  - Draft journal entries to (i) reverse the incorrect entries, including the one to the suspense account and (ii) make the correct entries

  - Enter the journals to clear the suspense account then

  - Redraft the trial balance

Keywords

Balance omission – a ledger account balance has been left out of the trial balance completely

Balance transfer error – either the wrong figure for a balance has been entered on the trial balance, or it has been entered on the wrong side of the trial balance

Calculation error – a mistake is made in calculating the balance on a ledger account

Compensating error – two separate errors that completely cancel each other out

Error of commission – the double entry is arithmetically correct but one of the entries has been made to the wrong account, though an account of the correct type

Error of omission – both the debit and credit entries have been omitted from the ledger accounts

Error of original entry – both the debit and credit entries in the ledgers have been made at the wrong amount

Error of principle – the double entry is arithmetically correct but one of the entries has been to the wrong type of account

Error of reversal of entries – the debit and credit entries have been reversed in the ledger accounts

Single entry error – only one side of the double entry has been made

Suspense account – opened in order to make the balances on a trial balance equal while the reason for the imbalance is discovered and corrected

Transposition error – the digits in a number are transposed (swapped round)

Two debits/two credits error – instead of a debit and a credit entry, either two debits or two credits have been made

Unequal amounts error – debit and credit entries have been made for different amounts

TEST YOUR LEARNING

Test 1

A payment for rent of £4,300 has been entered into the cash book and the rent account as £3,400. What type of error is this?

Test 2

The sales returns for a period of £1,276 have been entered into the ledger accounts as:

DR   Sales ledger control
CR   Sales returns

What type of error has taken place?

Test 3

A credit note from supplier Hamish & Co has been debited to the account of C Hamish. What type of error is this?

Test 4

The total of the debit balances on a trial balance are £325,778 and the total of the credit balances are £326,048. What would be one of the first types of error that you might look for?

Test 5

The total of the debit balances on a trial balance was £452,362 and the credit side totalled £450,241. What is the balance on the suspense account?

£		Credit balance/
		Debit balance

Test 6

The total of the debit balances on a trial balance was £184,266 and the credit side totalled £181,278. The business does not maintain Cash control or Bank control accounts in the general ledger. The following errors were discovered:

(a) A receipt of £3,250 from a customer was recorded in the Cash Book correctly but in the sales ledger control account as £2,350.

(b) The discounts allowed account was overcast by £1,000 when being balanced prior to its entry in the trial balance.

(c) Discounts received of £450 were debited to the discounts received account and credited to the purchases ledger control account.

(d) Purchases returns of £1,088 had been correctly entered in the purchases ledger control account but had been omitted from the purchases returns account.

Draft journal entries to remove the incorrect entries for each of these errors and make the correct ones, and show how the suspense account is cleared.

Account name	Amount £	Debit ✓	Credit ✓

Suspense account

	£		£

Test 7

Alvescot Co's trial balance was extracted and did not balance. The debit column of the trial balance totalled £52,673 and the credit column totalled £61,920.

(a) What entry would be made in the suspense account to balance the trial balance?

Account name	Amount £	Debit ✓	Credit ✓
Suspense			

(b) It is important to understand the types of error that are disclosed by the trial balance and those that are not.

Show which of the errors below are, or are not, disclosed by the trial balance.

Error in the general ledger	Error disclosed by the trial balance ✓	Error NOT disclosed by the trial balance ✓
Calculating the balance on a ledger account incorrectly by £100		
Recording a supplier's credit note for £800 at £80 in the purchases returns day book		
Forgetting to include the £200 balance on the petty cash book in the trial balance		
Making the debit entry for a cash sale of £150 but not the credit entry		
Failing to record a petty cash purchase of food for £20 (no VAT)		
For a purchase of stationery on credit, debiting the PLCA and crediting the stationery account		

Test 8

The initial trial balance of a business includes a suspense account with a balance of £1,000.

The error has been traced to the casting of the net column of the purchases day book shown below.

Purchases Day Book

Date 20XX	Details	Invoice number	Total £	VAT £	Net £
31 Oct	Hughson Ltd	1902	1,740	290	1,450
31 Oct	Rundle Co	43902	432	72	360
31 Oct	Westcot Jenks	6327	2,562	427	2,135
	Totals		4,734	789	4,945

(a) Using the picklist of account names, record the journal entries needed in the general ledger to:

(i) Remove the amount entered incorrectly.

Account name	Amount £	Debit ✓	Credit ✓

(ii) Record the correct entry.

Account name	Amount £	Debit ✓	Credit ✓

(iii) Remove the suspense account balance.

Account name	Amount £	Debit ✓	Credit ✓

Picklist of account names:

Hughson Ltd
Purchases
Purchases day book
Purchases ledger control
Purchases returns
Purchases returns day book
Rundle Co

Sales
Sales day book
Sales ledger control
Sales returns
Sales returns day book
Suspense
VAT
Westcot Jenks

(b) An entry to record purchases of goods on credit for £980 (no VAT) has been reversed. Using the picklist of account names, record the journal entries needed in the general ledger to:

(i) Remove the incorrect entries.

Account name	Amount £	Debit ✓	Credit ✓

(ii) Record the correct entries.

Account name	Amount £	Debit ✓	Credit ✓

Picklist of account names:

Bank
Cash
Purchases
Purchases ledger control
Sales
Sales ledger control
Suspense
VAT

Test 9

The initial trial balance of a business included a suspense account. All the bookkeeping errors have now been traced and the journal entries shown below have been recorded.

Journal entries

Account name	Debit £	Credit £
Discounts allowed	149	
Discounts received		149
Suspense	256	
Purchases		256
Motor expenses	893	
Suspense		893

Post the journal entries to the general ledger accounts. Dates are not required.

Purchases

Details	Amount £	Details	Amount £

Motor expenses

Details	Amount £	Details	Amount £

Suspense

Details	Amount £	Details	Amount £
Balance b/f	637		

Discounts received

Details	Amount £	Details	Amount £

Discounts allowed

Details	Amount £	Details	Amount £

Picklist of account names:

Balance b/f
Discounts allowed
Discounts received
Motor expenses
Purchases
Suspense

Test 10

On 31 March a business extracted an initial trial balance which did not balance as the debit balances exceeded the credit balances by £1,148. On 1 April journal entries were prepared to correct the errors that had been found, and clear the suspense account. The list of balances in the initial trial balance, and the journal entries to correct the errors, are shown below. The journals had not yet been entered when the account balances were extracted.

Taking into account the journal entries, which will clear the suspense account, re-draft the trial balance by placing the figures in the debit or credit column.

	Balances extracted on 31 March £	Balances at 1 April	
		Debit £	Credit £
Machinery	52,910		
Fixtures and fittings	17,835		
Computers	9,920		
Cash at bank	2,367		
Petty cash	250		
Sales ledger control	115,438		
Purchases ledger control	34,290		
VAT (owing to HM Revenue & Customs)	2,337		
Capital	52,254		
Sales	270,256		
Purchases	78,309		
Purchases returns	3,203		
Wages	54,219		
Maintenance expenses	3,445		
Administration expenses	10,254		
Marketing expenses	6,287		
Premises expenses	15,244		
Discounts received	4,278		
Discounts allowed	1,288		
Totals			

Journal entries

Account name	Debit £	Credit £
Discounts allowed		1,359
Suspense	1,359	
Discounts allowed	1,539	
Suspense		1,539

Account name	Debit £	Credit £
Purchases ledger control		664
Suspense	664	
Purchases ledger control		664
Suspense	664	

chapter 6:
THE BANKING SYSTEM

chapter coverage 📖

In this final chapter we cover how the banking system works and the way in which receipts are checked. The topics covered are:

- ✍ Banking services
- ✍ Availability of money banked
- ✍ Retaining banking documentation
- ✍ Making payment by cheque
- ✍ Checking payments received by cheque
- ✍ Checking payments received by credit card
- ✍ Checking payments received by debit card
- ✍ Paying in cash and cheques to the bank

BANKING SERVICES

Most people and businesses have a bank account so that they do not have to keep all their money only as cash. The problems with holding money as cash are that:

- It poses a security risk
- It earns no interest
- It is difficult to use as a means of payment except in face-to-face transactions

Due to immense competition between financial institutions in recent years, banks and large building societies now offer a vast array of services to customers. These services fall into four main categories:

HOLDING money for customers	Making PAYMENTS for customers
Providing LOANS	OTHER services

Building societies are owned by their customers, who are referred to as 'members'. Member-owned mutual building societies, as distinct from shareholder-owned banks, historically had concentrated only on:

- Holding money for members in savings accounts, and
- Providing mortgage loans to members

While some small building societies still focus only on these areas, perhaps providing foreign currency and insurance services in addition, the big ones operate in all areas of banking services, including providing overdrafts, personal loans, credit cards, business banking and safe custody.

In this chapter we will use the term 'bank' to refer to all the large financial institutions that provide all these services, including corporate services to businesses, and the term 'building society' to refer to the small building societies that still operate at a restricted level, primarily holding money for individual savers and providing mortgages to individual borrowers.

Holding money

Most banks offer a variety of different types of bank account to suit all customers' needs. The most commonly used is a CURRENT ACCOUNT (sometimes called a CHEQUE ACCOUNT) whereby customers pay money into the account and can then draw on it. Customers can access their money by:

- Writing CHEQUES (a cheque is 'a written order to the bank (the drawee), signed by the bank's customer (the drawer) to pay a certain amount, specified in words and figures, to another specified person (the drawee)'. We shall come back to cheques later in this chapter

- Withdrawing cash at the counter or from Automatic Teller Machines (ATMs)

- Arranging automated payments from the account – we saw various types of automated payment in Chapter 1, namely bank giro credits (BGC), BACS transfers, CHAPS transfers, Faster Payments, standing orders and direct debits

- Using their DEBIT CARD to make payment in a shop or over the phone or internet (we shall come back to debit cards later in this chapter)

Many current accounts attract a (very low) rate of interest on a positive balance.

A customer can also choose to save money at a higher interest rate by paying money into a DEPOSIT ACCOUNT. This will not normally have a cheque book or a debit card but will generally pay a higher rate of interest than a current account. Some deposit accounts pay even higher rates of interest but restrict the movement of money, for example a withdrawal of money may require one month's notice.

Making payments

Banks have a duty to pay cheques that are correctly written out by customers provided they have enough money in their account, or an overdraft authorised to cover the amount. If they do not have sufficient money then banks may dishonour or return cheques unpaid. The person who took the cheque in settlement of a debt must then find another way to obtain payment from the bank's customer.

To overcome this uncertainty many banks, in return for a fee, will provide customers with a BANK DRAFT, which is essentially a non-cancellable cheque drawn on the bank itself rather than on the customer's account. A bank draft gives the recipient of it complete confidence that they will receive payment when it is presented to the bank. It is therefore often used in large transactions between individuals, for instance when one person (A) buys a car from another (B): A hands B the draft and drives the car away, which B is happy to allow as B knows that the draft will be honoured by the bank on which it is drawn.

The banks also offer the service of making and receiving automated payments out of and into an account by other means such as standing orders, direct debits, BACS, CHAPS and other automated payments, including online transfers using the Faster Payments service. The banks must collect payment for cheques that the customer pays into the bank account, and will accept transfers from other bank accounts.

Providing loans

Banks can provide loans to both personal and business customers, in a number of different ways.

Many current accounts have an agreed OVERDRAFT FACILITY whereby a customer can authorise payments for more than the positive balance on the account up to a certain amount and these will still be paid. A fairly high rate of interest is usually charged for this facility, so it is only appropriate for use as a short-term loan of variable amounts.

A further method by which banks and other financial institutions can provide short-term loans to customers is by issuing CREDIT CARDS. These allow customers to make purchases and to defer payment until some future time. The balance on the credit card account does not have to be paid off each month, only a minimum sum is necessary. Any outstanding balances on these credit card accounts usually attract a very high rate of interest. It is important to remember that **a person's credit card transactions have no direct effect on their current account at their bank** – the current account is affected by the person's debit card transactions, but not by payments they make using any credit card they possess. Credit card transactions are reflected in a totally separate credit card account with a credit card company, which is usually a bank.

Banks can provide medium to long-term LOANS to both personal and business customers with various terms and conditions and repayment terms. A loan is usually of a fixed amount.

Banks also provide MORTGAGES, which are long-term loans repayable over 25 years, in order for an individual (and sometimes a business) to purchase a property. The mortgage is secured on the property. This means that if the loan is not repaid for some reason then the bank ultimately has an enforceable right to sell the property in order to get its money back.

Other services

Banks also provide a number of other services that can be of use to businesses:

- Provision of a nightsafe (so the business can deposit cash and cheques at the bank even after it has closed for the day)

- Supplying foreign currency

- Making safe custody boxes available for safekeeping of valuable items such as documents

- Investment advice

- Insurance products

- Corporate credit cards

Task 1

A sole trader is setting up in business with £50,000. He hopes that only £30,000 of this will be initially required for trading transactions and that the remainder can be saved for future growth. What type of bank account would be best suited for the remaining £20,000 for this trader?

AVAILABILITY OF MONEY BANKED

If you write out a cheque then the eventual outcome is that the money will be paid out of your bank account by your bank and paid into the account of the payee of the cheque. However, in order for this to happen to the many thousands of cheques that are written each day a complex system is in operation. This cheque CLEARING SYSTEM was set up by the major banks. It takes three working days for a customer's cheque paid by a business into its bank account to clear from the customer's account into its account and therefore to be available as money that the business can draw on.

While a business which pays a customer's cheque into its bank on Day 1 will have to wait until Day 4 to be able to draw that money out again, if it pays in cash (notes and coins) this money is generally available immediately. Furthermore, many automated payments can be made and accessed very quickly if the person making the payment has a bank which operates the Faster Payments system.

Customer payments by debit card and credit card are nearly always made via online card machines so the money is available to the supplier instantaneously.

RETAINING BANKING DOCUMENTATION

When dealing with its bank a business will handle a large number of different types of document. They are all important and document retention should therefore be dealt with carefully. For reasons of tax compliance and because they are used as primary documents which are recorded in the books of prime entry, the business should have a DOCUMENT RETENTION POLICY which requires that the following documentation should be retained for at least six years:

- Bank statements
- Paying-in slip stubs and other receipts for amounts paid into the bank
- Cheque book stubs
- Standing order and direct debit schedules
- Confirmations of instructions to make Faster Payments and other online transfers
- Instructions to make BACS and CHAPS payments

The document retention policy should be in writing and should be updated regularly to keep pace with changes in banking products and the organisation's procedures. As well as specifying what should be retained and for how long, the policy should also set out the form in which the documents should be retained. This may be in paper form, in the case of paying-in slips and cheque book stubs for example, or electronic form in the case of debit and credit card receipts and authorised BACS payments.

The document retention policy may also include guidance on how confidential documents should be disposed of if they are not to be retained in that form, for instance if only electronic copies are to be retained long-term. The best method is to use a shredder to shred the original hard copies so there is no possibility of the information falling into the wrong hands. Obviously it is very important however that shredding should only take place once a proper electronic copy has been made.

We have seen some details relating to automated payments in Chapter 1. In this chapter we concentrate on making payment by cheque and on checking payments received by cheque, debit card and credit card (and cash) to ensure they are valid.

MAKING PAYMENT BY CHEQUE

Cheques are likely to be phased out as a payment method in the UK by 2018 but are currently still used in many transactions between individuals and, sometimes, between individuals and businesses.

When opening an account with a bank a business is issued with a cheque book which contains pre-printed, sequentially numbered cheques. It is important to keep cheque books securely, ideally in a safe. When a business writes out a cheque made payable to a supplier it is instructing its bank to pay the supplier the amount of the cheque from the business's bank account.

There are three parties involved in a cheque from a customer to a supplier:

- The DRAWER – the person who is writing and signing the cheque in order to make a payment (ie the customer)

- The DRAWEE – the bank who has issued the cheque and will have to pay the cheque (ie the customer's bank)

- The PAYEE – the person to whom the cheque is being paid (ie the supplier)

Increasingly, retailers and a business's regular suppliers are reluctant to accept cheques as payment, and indeed many businesses prefer to make automated payments. However, cheques are still regularly used so you need to be aware of the procedures that relate to them.

A typical cheque and its CHEQUE BOOK STUB or COUNTERFOIL (the part of the document that is retained by the business writing out the cheque as its primary record) is shown below, together with an indication of what each of the details on the face of the cheque means.

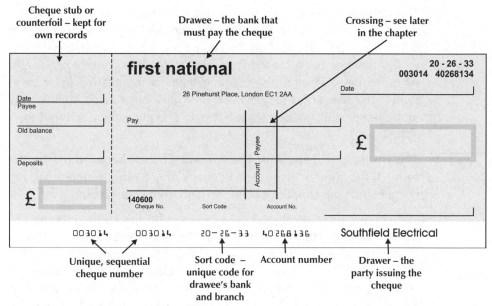

Many cheques issued by businesses are produced by their computerised accounting systems so all the details are printed on them, though cheques completed by hand are still often used. However it is completed, a cheque must be filled out properly (as illustrated below) and checks carried out to ensure accuracy.

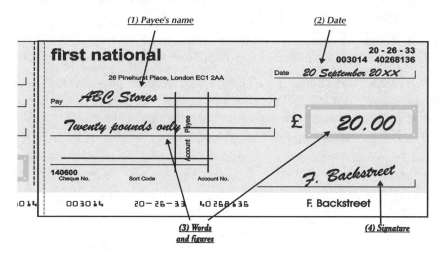

(1) The **payee's name**, ie your supplier, must be correct. For many shops which still accept cheques this is not relevant as they offer to stamp their customers' cheques with the organisation's name rather than the customer having to write it out.

(2) The **date** must be today's date. A cheque should not be dated later than today's date as it cannot be paid into the supplier's account until the date on the cheque. Also the cheque must not have an earlier date on it. A cheque has a limited life and it is common banking practice to refuse to pay a cheque that is more than six months old in order to protect the drawer, as the payment may have been made another way in the intervening period. An out-of-date cheque is often referred to as 'stale'.

(3) The **words and figures for the amount of the cheque must be the same**. If they do not agree then the bank may return or 'dishonour' the cheque and your supplier will not be paid from your account.

(4) The cheque must be **signed** by a person who has been authorised to do so (an AUTHORISED SIGNATORY). Most organisations have a written agreement with their bank about who is allowed to sign the organisation's cheques as part of the necessary security procedures for cheque payments. The bank will only accept cheques that have been signed by the correct people. In many organisations there will be monetary limits set on cheque signatures. For example, a business operating as a company may have a policy where the signature of just one director is required for cheques up to a value of £8,000, but if the cheque is for more than this amount then two directors' signatures are required.

The date, supplier and amount must be written onto the cheque book stub for the cheque, as this is the primary record from which the Cash Book is written up.

The two parallel vertical lines on a cheque with **Account payee** written between them are known as a CROSSING. This means that the cheque can only be paid into the bank account of the payee on the cheque, ie into ABC Stores' bank account. This is another important security procedure for cheque payments.

HOW IT WORKS

Southfield Electrical is making a payment to a supplier, Grangemouth Supplies, of £783.60 after deducting a settlement discount of £23.50. The cheque and stub are shown below:

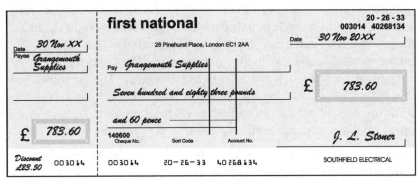

Note that where there are any blank spaces on the cheque, for example after writing the amount in words, a line is drawn through the space as a security procedure to minimise the chances of the cheque being fraudulently altered.

If an error is made when writing out the cheque it should be amended and then initialled by the authorised signatory. Alternatively the cheque should be destroyed and a new one written out. In this case a note should be made on the destroyed cheque's counterfoil to the effect that the cheque has not been issued.

If the business chooses to give a bank draft rather than a simple cheque in paying a supplier, it must ask its bank to draw a cheque on itself, which it will do if the business has sufficient money to cover the payment and is willing to pay a fee. Both the drawer and the drawee of a bank draft is the bank. Bank drafts are used to give the supplier an absolute guarantee that they will receive payment for the amount of the draft, as they cannot be cancelled or dishonoured.

CHECKING PAYMENTS RECEIVED BY CHEQUE

When a customer sends in a cheque in payment of their debt it is important to check the details carefully:

- Check that there is a signature on the cheque and that this agrees with the account name printed on the cheque, if it is a personal cheque. This may be difficult however if the signature is unreadable, as is often the case!

- Check that the cheque has been completed properly in terms of payee name, the date, and that the words and figures agree with each other.

CHECKING PAYMENTS RECEIVED BY CREDIT CARD

A further common method of paying for goods is by CREDIT CARD. A customer must apply to a credit card company for a credit card, and upon its issue a credit card limit (which cannot be exceeded) is set for the customer. The customer can pay for goods and services with the credit card at outlets that accept credit card payments. At the end of each month the customer is sent a credit card statement showing: all of the purchases on the credit card for the month; the total outstanding on the credit card; the minimum payment required; the date by which payment should reach the credit card company. The customer can then choose whether to pay off the full amount outstanding on the account or only part of it. Any unpaid outstanding amount will have interest charged on it which will appear on the next credit card statement.

A business which accepts payment by credit card from customers will have to pay the credit card company a percentage commission on transactions (normally between 1% and 4%) for the right to do so.

A typical credit card is shown below.

When accepting a credit card as payment the retailer will usually process it through an electronic card machine attached to an electronic till. The card machine is connected online to the credit card company. In some businesses, such as restaurants, the retailer keys in the transaction total to the card machine, but usually this is done electronically by the attached till (see below).

Electronic payment by credit card

The credit card is inserted in the card machine, which contains the transaction total transmitted to it by the till. The card machine reads the credit card details off the chip in the card. The following checks are carried out, mostly by the card machine via the online connection to the credit card company:

- The retailer runs their finger over the card's signature strip to check that the card has not been tampered with (this is only possible if the retailer actually holds the card at some point; this is increasingly uncommon in practice as customers insert their cards direct into the card machine).

- When the card is inserted, the card machine automatically checks:

    - That the card has not expired and is not stolen

    - That the transaction total does not take the customer over his or her credit card limit

- The customer enters their Personal Identification Number (PIN) into the card machine's keypad to confirm the transaction and their identity.

- The credit card company authorises the transaction online and provides the authorisation code.

- The card machine produces a two-part card receipt. The top copy is given to the customer, along with a separate VAT receipt produced by the electronic till, and the other copy of the card receipt is retained by the retailer.

- Very occasionally, the customer may be asked for further authentication by signing the card receipt.

- The transaction total is automatically charged to the customer's credit card account and credited to the retailer's bank account by electronic funds transfer at point of sale (EFTPOS).

Telephone payment by credit card

If a business takes credit card payments over the phone from customers it is important that the correct information is obtained from the customer so the

transaction can be checked. With reference to the credit card he or she should be asked for:

- The credit card account number embossed as a 16 digit number across the front of the card

- The expiry date on the card, for instance 05/16

- The exact name of the cardholder as embossed on the front of the card

- The last three digits of the number printed on the signature strip on the reverse of the card – this is the card's SECURITY NUMBER

There is no need to ask for the 'valid from' date nor for the issue number which is printed on the front of the card in some cases.

The business keys the information in to its system and the same checks are then made by the credit card company as detailed above.

It is completely inappropriate to ask the customer for either the credit limit on the credit card account or for the Personal Identification Number (PIN) which the customer uses when making cash withdrawals at ATMs or payments in shops. This is highly confidential information which the business has no right or need to know.

CHECKING PAYMENTS RECEIVED BY DEBIT CARD

Most banks provide their current account customers with a DEBIT CARD. These look very similar to credit cards but their nature and purpose is very different. When a debit card is used to pay for a transaction, the amount is **automatically deducted from the customer's bank account** by EFTPOS and added to the supplier's bank account.

The procedure for processing and checking a debit card as payment in an electronic transaction is the same as that for a credit card, except that the card machine is connected online with the customer's bank rather than with their credit card company. An additional check is that the bank ensures the transaction date is after the issue date that is printed on the front of the debit card, ie it checks that the card is current.

If a business takes debit card payments over the phone from customers, the same information is required from the customer as for a credit card transaction: the debit card account number, the expiry date, the exact name of the cardholder on the front of the card and the security number. In addition, for some debit cards the issue number and 'valid from' date is required, so that the bank can be sure the card is current. It is inappropriate to ask the customer for any other information, particularly the PIN.

Task 2

What is the essential difference between a credit card and a debit card?

PAYING IN CASH AND CHEQUES TO THE BANK

As we have seen many businesses, and in particular retailers, receive payments from their customers in cash and by cheque. Cash and cheques are paid in at the bank's counter using a PAYING-IN SLIP. As we saw in Chapter 1, such payments in of money appear as a 'counter credit' on the bank statement.

When opening an account with a bank a business is issued with a paying-in book which contains pre-printed, sequentially numbered paying-in slips. A typical paying-in slip plus the PAYING-IN SLIP STUB (to the left) is shown below – note how both front and back are shown as both sides need to be completed in detail.

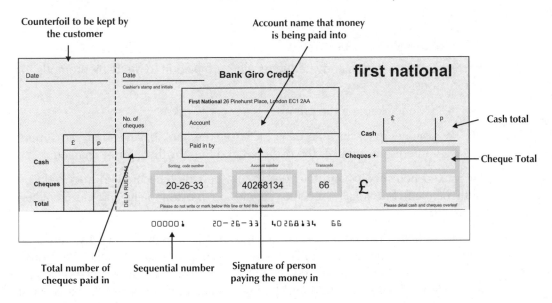

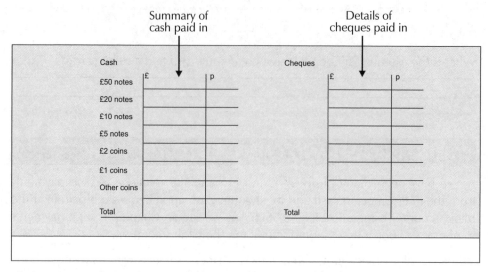

The paying-in slip itself is handed at the bank's counter together with the cash and cheques. The paying-in slip stub is retained in the paying-in book and is the primary record for what is entered in the Cash Book.

Security procedures for receipts

It is important that cash and cheque receipts are paid in to the bank promptly for two reasons:

- Money kept on the premises is a security risk.

- Money paid into the bank increases the bank balance and earns more interest, or reduces the overdraft and thereby the interest charged.

Unbanked notes, coins and cheques should be stored securely in a locked safe until banked, but ideally receipts should be banked daily and not retained overnight.

When actually transporting cash to the bank, **personal security** must be considered. It might be advisable for two members of staff to take the money together or to employ a security firm if the amount of cash is large. It is also advisable to change the route and timing of bank visits on a regular basis. Most importantly, the details of bank paying-in visits must be treated with the highest confidentiality.

Often a business, particularly a retailer, needs to pay money into the bank when the bank itself is shut. Many bank branches provide a **nightsafe** for this purpose. A nightsafe is normally a safe with access from the outer wall of the bank where the money and paying-in slip can be placed in a special wallet which travels down a chute into the bank itself.

CHAPTER OVERVIEW

- Banks provide a variety of different types of account that customers can use such as current accounts and deposit accounts

- Banks have a duty to pay cheques that customers have correctly drawn up provided there is enough money in the customer's account, or a sufficient overdraft limit

- Banks must honour a bank draft drawn on the bank by itself at its customer's request

- Banks provide overdraft facilities to customers, credit cards, loans and mortgages

- Building societies are typically small organisations that provide mortgages and savings products for their members

- The clearing system means it takes three working days for a cheque to be available as money after being paid into a bank

- When a business accepts a credit or debit card as payment an online card machine makes automatic checks on whether the card is current/has expired/has been stolen and whether the transaction total takes the customer over his or her limit

- Customer payments by credit card are automatically entered on the customer's credit card account and added to the business's bank account

- Customer payments by debit card are automatically deducted from the customer's bank account and added to the business's bank account

- Cheques and cash received should be paid into the bank promptly. Great care must be taken when taking large amounts to the bank – ideally two people should be taking the money and using varying routes at different times of day

Keywords

Authorised signatory – a person authorised to sign a cheque

Bank draft – non-cancellable cheque drawn on the bank rather than the customer's account

Cheque – a customer's written order to their bank to pay a specified sum to a particular person's bank account

Cheque book stub – the part of the cheque that is retained by the drawer as its primary record

Clearing system – the system set up by the major banks to deal with the payment of cheques which means there is a three day delay between paying a cheque into an account and being able to access the money

Credit card – a card which allows the customer to purchase goods and services on credit now but gives them flexibility as to when they repay the credit card company

Credit card security number – three digit security number printed on the signature strip on the reverse of a credit card or debit card

Crossing – the two parallel vertical lines on a cheque with 'Account payee' written between them to ensure that the cheque can only be paid into the bank account of the payee

Current account – a bank account designed to have money withdrawn by cheque or other methods on a regular basis

Debit card – a card which allows the customer to purchase goods and services where the sale is automatically debited to the customer's bank account and credited to the supplier's bank account

Deposit account – an account from which it is not intended to make regular withdrawals (a savings account)

Document retention policy – a written policy prepared by the business which sets out which items of documentation relating to banking should be retained, how it should be retained and for how long

Drawee – the bank who has issued the cheque and will have to pay the cheque

Drawer – the person who is writing and signing the cheque in order to make a payment (ie the customer)

Loan – an advance from a bank on which interest will be charged and repayment conditions laid down

Mortgage – a long-term loan for purchase of a property under which the property serves as security for the loan

Overdraft facility – an agreement that the customer can withdraw more money from the current account than they have in it, up to a certain limit

Payee – the person to whom the cheque is being paid (ie the supplier)

Paying-in slip – a pre-printed, sequentially numbered document for paying cash and cheques into the bank

Paying-in slip stub – the part of the paying in slip that is retained by the business as its primary record of cash and cheques paid into the bank

TEST YOUR LEARNING

Test 1

Identify whether each of the statements below is True or False.

	True ✓	False ✓
A bank draft cannot be cancelled once it has been issued		
Any customer who pays with a debit card is taking out a loan with its bank as a result		

BPP
LEARNING MEDIA

ANSWERS TO CHAPTER TASKS

CHAPTER 1 Bank reconciliations

1 A credit balance

2 Debit side of the cash book

3 Credit side of the cash book

4 As an unpresented cheque

5 Credit

6 £1,441.93 debit balance

CHAPTER 2 Introduction to control accounts

1 Debit Sales ledger control

   Credit Sales/VAT

2 Debit Purchases/VAT

   Credit Purchases ledger control

CHAPTER 3 Preparing and reconciling control accounts

1 Debit Irrecoverable debts expense

   Debit VAT control

   Credit Sales ledger control

2 The sales ledger control account

3 If the total of the discounts allowed column from the Cash Book of £300 was not posted for a period, this would be adjusted for in the sales ledger control account reconciliation by subtracting £300 from the sales ledger control account balance

4 The purchases ledger control account

5 An invoice for £200 was entered into the individual account in the purchases ledger on the wrong side of the account. This would be adjusted

for in the purchases ledger control account reconciliation by adding £400 to the list of purchases ledger balances.

CHAPTER 4 The journal

1   £294.50 (400.00 – 69.00 – 34.00 – 2.50)

2   The HMRC account = £143 (69 + 33 + 41)

Wages expense account = £441 (400 + 41)

CHAPTER 5 Errors and the trial balance

1   This is a transposition error which will cause an imbalance in the trial balance.

2   Unequal amounts error; balance transfer error; error of original entry

3   A commission error

4

Account name	Amount £	Debit	Credit
Reversing entries:			
Bank	1,250		✓
Sales ledger control	1,250		✓
Suspense	2,500	✓	
Correcting entries:			
Bank	1,250	✓	
Sales ledger control	1,250		✓

CHAPTER 6 The banking system

1   Deposit account

2   Debit cards immediately reduce the bank account balance of the customer. Credit is given for credit cards.

TEST YOUR LEARNING – ANSWERS

CHAPTER 1   Bank reconciliations

Test 1

Cash book – debit side

Date	Details	Ref	Discounts allowed £	Bank £	Trade receivables £
30/11	Burser Ltd	SL14	6.49	147.89	147.89
30/11	Crawley Partners	SL23	18.79	448.36	448.36
30/11	Breon & Co	SL15		273.37	273.37
30/11	Kogart Supplies	SL06	42.67	552.68	552.68
30/11	Alex & Bros	SL09		273.46	273.46
30/11	Minicar Ltd	SL22		194.68	194.68

Cash book – credit side

Date	Details	Ref	Discounts received £	Bank £	Trade payables £	Sundry £
27/11	SO Loan Fin Rep	ML23		250.00		250.00
30/11	Waterloo Partners 001367	PL21	12.47	336.47	336.47	
30/11	Central Supplies 001368	PL16		169.36	169.36	
30/11	Gen Lon Trade 001369	PL23	10.58	268.38	268.38	
30/11	Eye of the Tiger 001370	PL19		84.50	84.50	
30/11	Chare & Cope 001371	PL27	19.86	447.39	447.39	

Test 2

Cash book – debit side

Date	Details	Ref	Discounts allowed £	Bank £	Trade receivables £
30/11	Burser Ltd	SL14	6.49	147.89✓	147.89
30/11	Crawley Partners	SL23	18.79	448.36✓	448.36
30/11	Breon & Co	SL15		273.37	273.37
30/11	Kogart Supplies	SL06	42.67	552.68✓	552.68
30/11	Alex & Bros	SL09		273.46	273.46
30/11	Minicar Ltd	SL22		194.68	194.68

Cash book – credit side

Date	Details	Ref	Discounts received £	Bank £	Trade payables £	Sundry £
27/11	SO Loan Fin Rep	ML23		250.00✓		250.00
30/11	Waterloo Part 001367	PL21	12.47	336.47✓	336.47	
30/11	Central Supp 001368	PL16		169.36	169.36	
30/11	Gen Lon Tr 001369	PL23	10.58	268.38	268.38	
30/11	Eye of the Tig 001370	PL19		84.50	84.50	
30/11	Chare & Cope 001371	PL27	19.86	447.39	447.39	

STATEMENT

NATIONAL DIRECT

THAMES TRADERS

CHEQUE ACCOUNT

Account number: 15-20-40 10267432

Date	Sheet 136	Paid out	Paid in	Balance
23.11	Balance b/f			1,489.65 C
26.11	Bank Giro Credit – Burser Ltd		52.00	1,541.65 C
27.11	SO-Loan Finance Repayment	250.00 ✓		1,291.65 C
28.11	Cheque No 001367 Counter credit	336.47 ✓	147.89 ✓	1,103.07 C
29.11	Cheque No 001368 Counter credit	196.36	448.36 ✓	1,355.07 C
30.11	Counter Credit Bank charges	34.53	552.68 ✓	1,873.22 C

Unticked items in the cash book

- The entries in the debit side of the cash book are cheques that have been paid into the bank but have not yet cleared – they will be agreed to subsequent bank statements

- Cheque no. 001368 – this cheque appeared as £169.36 in the cash book but as £196.36 in the bank statement – this should be checked to the original cheque stub and documentation and if the bank is correct the cash book must be adjusted

- The remaining cheque payments in the cash book have not yet cleared the banking system and they will be checked to subsequent bank statements

Unticked items in the bank statement

- 26/11 bank giro credit from Burser Ltd – this has not been entered into the cash book yet so it must therefore be adjusted to reflect this

- 29/11 – cheque no. 001368 – as has already been noted, this has been incorrectly entered into the cash book and must be adjusted for

- 30/11 – bank charges – these have not been entered into the cash book and this must be adjusted for

Test 3

Cash book – debit side

Date	Details	Ref	Discounts allowed	Bank	Trade receivables
			£	£	£
30/11	Burser Ltd	SL14	6.49	147.89✓	147.89
30/11	Crawley Partners	SL23	18.79	448.36✓	448.36
30/11	Breon & Co	SL15		273.37	273.37
30/11	Kogart Supplies	SL06	42.67	552.68✓	552.68
30/11	Alex & Bros	SL09		273.46	273.46
30/11	Minicar Ltd	SL22		194.68	194.68
30/11	Burser Ltd BGC	SL14		52.00✓	52.00
			67.95	1,942.44	1,942.44

Cash book – credit side

Date	Details	Ref	Discounts received £	Bank £	Trade payables £	Sundry £
27/11	SO Loan Fin Rep	ML2 3		250.00✓		250.00
30/11	Waterloo Part 001367	PL21	12.47	336.47✓	336.47	
30/11	Central Supp 001368	PL16		169.36✓	169.36	
30/11	Gen Lon Tr 001369	PL23	10.58	268.38	268.38	
30/11	Eye of the Tig 001370	PL19		84.50	84.50	
30/11	Chare & Cope 001371	PL27	19.86	447.39	447.39	
30/11	Adjustment to 001368	PL16		27.00✓	27.00	
30/11	Bank charges	GL		34.53✓		34.53
			42.91	1,617.63	1,333.10	284.53

Note that the amount £169.36 (cheque no. 1368) can now be ticked because the adjustment of £27 means that both entries total the amount (£196.36) ticked on the bank statement.

Test 4

	£
Opening balance	1,489.65
Add receipts for the period	1,942.44
Less payments for the period	(1,617.63)
Bank account trial balance figure at 30 November	1,814.46

Test 5

Bank reconciliation statement as at 30 November

	£
Balance per bank statement	1,873.22
Add:	
Breon & Co	273.37
Alex & Bros	273.46
Minicar Ltd	194.68
Total to add:	741.51
Less:	
001369	268.38
001370	84.50
001371	447.39
Total to subtract:	(800.27)
Balance as per correct, adjusted cash book	1,814.46

Test 6

Cash book

Date 20XX	Details	Bank £	Date 20XX	Cheque number	Details	Bank £
01 Feb	Balance b/f	6,230	01 Feb	003252	Jeggers Ltd	2,567
20 Feb	Straightens Co	2,228	01 Feb	003253	Short & Fell	333
21 Feb	Plumpers	925	01 Feb	003254	Rastop Ltd	1,006
22 Feb	Eastern Supplies	1,743	01 Feb	003255	A & D Trading	966
09 Feb	Branthill Co	1,559	02 Feb	003256	Jesmond Warr	2,309
			02 Feb	003257	Nistral Ltd	3,775
			13 Feb	003258	Simpsons	449
			13 Feb		AxDC	250
			18 Feb		Trust Insurance	325
			20 Feb		Bank charges	14
			22 Feb		Interest charge	56
			23 Feb		Balance c/d	635
		12,685				12,685
24 Feb	Balance b/d	635				

Bank reconciliation statement as at 23 Feb 20XX

Balance per bank statement		£	725
Add:			
Name:	Plumpers	£	925
Name:	Eastern Supplies	£	1,743
Total to add		£	2,668
Less:			
Name:	Jesmond Warr	£	2,309
Name:	Simpsons	£	449
Total to subtract		£	2,758
Balance as per cash book		£	635

CHAPTER 2   Introduction to control accounts

Test 1

	Bank DR/CR	SLCA DR/CR	PLCA DR/CR	VAT DR/CR	Sales DR/CR	Purchases returns DR/CR	Discounts received DR/CR	Discounts allowed DR/CR
Gross sales		DR		CR	CR			
Gross purchases returns			DR	CR		CR		
Discounts allowed		CR						DR
Discounts received			DR				CR	
Gross payments from cash customers	DR			CR	CR			
Payments to credit suppliers	CR		DR					

Test 2

General ledger

Sales ledger control account

	£		£
Balance b/f	1,216.26	Bank	1,078.97
Sales	1,636.20	Discounts allowed	8.73
		Balance c/d	1,764.76
	2,852.46		2,852.46
Balance b/d	1,764.76		

Sales ledger

Virgo Partners

	£		£
Balance b/f	227.58	CB	117.38
SDB	96.72		
SDB	214.44	Balance c/d	421.36
	538.74		538.74
Balance b/d	421.36		

McGowan & Sons

	£		£
Balance b/f	552.73	CB	552.73
SDB	595.08	Balance c/d	595.08
	1,147.81		1,147.81
Balance b/d	595.08		

J J Westrope

	£		£
Balance b/f	317.59	CB	308.86
SDB	167.40	CB – discount	8.73
SDB	277.32	Balance c/d	444.72
	762.31		762.31
Balance b/d	444.72		

Jacks Ltd

	£		£
Balance b/f	118.36	CB	100.00
SDB	107.64		
SDB	177.60	Balance c/d	303.60
	403.60		403.60
Balance b/d	303.60		

Reconciliation

	£
Sales ledger control account balance as at 31 May	1,764.76
Total of sales ledger accounts as at 31 May (see workings)	1,764.76
Difference	0

Workings

	£
Virgo Partners	421.36
McGowan & Sons	595.08
J J Westrope	444.72
Jacks Ltd	303.60
Total	1,764.76

Test 3

General ledger

Purchases ledger control account

	£		£
Bank	959.39	Balance b/f	839.46
Discounts received	30.07	Purchases	1,606.92
Balance c/d	1,456.92		
	2,446.38		2,446.38
		Balance b/d	1,456.92

Purchases ledger

Jenkins Suppliers

	£		£
CB	423.89	Balance b/f	441.56
CB – discounts	17.67	PDB	219.96
Balance c/d	671.28	PDB	451.32
	1,112.84		1,112.84
		Balance b/d	671.28

Kilnfarm Paper

	£		£
CB	150.00	Balance b/f	150.00
CB	150.00	PDB	153.12
Balance c/d	156.24	PDB	153.12
	456.24		456.24
		Balance b/d	156.24

Barnfield Ltd

	£		£
CB	235.50	Balance b/f	247.90
CB – discounts	12.40	PDB	317.16
Balance c/d	629.40	PDB	312.24
	877.30		877.30
		Balance b/d	629.40

Reconciliation

	£
Purchases ledger control account balance as at 31 May	1,456.92
Total of purchases ledger accounts as at 31 May (see workings)	1,456.92
Difference	0

Workings

	£
Jenkins Suppliers	671.28
Kilnfarm Paper	156.24
Barnfield Ltd	629.40
Purchases ledger control account balance	1,456.92

CHAPTER 3 Preparing and reconciling control accounts

Test 1

Sales ledger control account

	£		£
Balance b/f	16,339	Sales returns	3,446
Sales	50,926	Bank	47,612
Bank (dishonoured cheque)	366	Discounts allowed	1,658
		Irrecoverable debts	500
		Balance c/d	14,415
	67,631		67,631

Test 2

Purchases ledger control account

	£		£
Purchases returns	2,568	Balance b/f	12,587
Bank	38,227	Purchases	40,827
Discounts received	998		
Balance c/d	11,621		
	53,414		53,414

Test 3

Sales ledger control account

	£		£
Balance b/f	41,774	Sales returns	450
Sales	100	Irrecoverable debts	210
		Balance c/d	41,214
	41,874		41,874
Balance b/d	41,214		

	£
Original total of list of balances	41,586
Less invoice misposted (769 – 679)	(90)
Less discount (2 × 16)	(32)
Less credit balance included as a debit balance (2 × 125)	(250)
Amended list of balances	41,214
Amended control account balance	41,214

Test 4

Purchases ledger control account

	£		£
Discount received	267	Balance b/f	38,694
		Purchases returns	300
Balance c/d	38,997	Bank (3,415 – 3,145)	270
	39,264		39,264
		Balance b/d	38,997

	£
Original total of list of balances	39,741
Less settlement discount omitted	(267)
Less credit note adjustment (210 – 120)	(90)
Less debit balance omitted	(187)
Less credit balance misstated	(200)
Amended list of balances	38,997
Amended control account balance	38,997

Test 5

(a)

Details	Amount £	Debit ✓	Credit ✓
Amount due to credit suppliers at 1 August	42,394		✓
Payments to credit suppliers	39,876	✓	
Purchases on credit	31,243		✓
Purchases returned to credit suppliers	1,266	✓	
Discounts received	501	✓	

(b)

	✓
Dr £31,994	
Cr £31,994	✓
Dr £34,526	
Cr £34,526	
Dr £32,996	
Cr £32,996	

(c)

	£
Purchases ledger control account balance as at 31 August	31,994
Total of purchases ledger accounts as at 31 August	32,190
Difference	196

(d)

	✓
A debit balance in the subsidiary ledger may have been included as a credit balance when calculating the total of the list of balances	✓
A credit balance in the subsidiary ledger may have been included as a debit balance when calculating the total of the list of balances	
A credit note may have been omitted from the purchases returns day book total	
Discounts received may only have been entered in the subsidiary ledger	

Test 6

(a)

VAT control

Details	Amount £	Details	Amount £
Purchases	14,368	Sales	29,072
Sales returns	858	Cash sales	332
		Purchases returns	488

(b)

15226   29882

	✓
Yes	
No	✓

The amount is owing **to** HMRC, not from HMRC.

CHAPTER 4   The journal

Test 1

Account name	Amount £	Debit	Credit
Capital	7,500		✓
Sales ledger control account	2,000	✓	
Purchases ledger control account	2,500		✓
Bank	8,000	✓	

Test 2

	Statutory deduction ✓	Voluntary deduction ✓
Pension contributions		✓
Income tax	✓	
Employee's NIC	✓	
Trade union fees		✓

Test 3

(a)

£	1,642.84

Workings

	£
Gross pay £27,000/12	2,250.00
PAYE income tax	(418.16)
Employee's NIC	(189.00)
Net pay	1,642.84

(b)

Wages control account

	£		£
Bank	1,642.84	Wages expense	2,250.00
HMRC	418.16	Wages expense	274.50
HMRC	189.00		
HMRC	274.50		

Wages expense account

	£		£
Wages control	2,250.00		
Wages control	274.50		

HMRC account

	£		£
		Wages control	418.16
		Wages control	189.00
		Wages control	274.50

Bank account

	£		£
		Wages control	1,642.84

Test 4

(a)

Account name	Amount £	Debit ✓	Credit ✓
Irrecoverable debts	1,290	✓	
VAT	258	✓	
Sales ledger control	1,548		✓

(b)

Account name	Amount £	Debit ✓	Credit ✓
Capital	18,410		✓
Cash at bank	3,270	✓	
Heat and light	300	✓	
Loan from bank	5,000		✓
Machinery	10,000	✓	
Motor vehicle	7,800	✓	
Petty cash	200	✓	
Rent paid	1,300	✓	
Stationery	190	✓	
Vehicle expenses	350	✓	
Journal to record the opening entries of new business			

Test 5

(a)

Account name	Amount £	Debit ✓	Credit ✓
Wages expense	13,776	✓	
Wages control	13,776		✓

(b)

Account name	Amount £	Debit ✓	Credit ✓
Wages control	3,698	✓	
HM Revenue & Customs	3,698		✓

(c)

Account name	Amount £	Debit ✓	Credit ✓
Wages control	9,978	✓	
Bank	9,978		✓

(d)

Account name	Amount £	Debit ✓	Credit ✓
Wages control	100	✓	
Loan	100		✓

CHAPTER 5   Errors and the trial balance

Test 1

Error of original entry (transposition error)

Test 2

Error of reversal of entries

Test 3

Error of commission

Test 4

Transposition error

The difference between the two figures (£270) is exactly divisible by 9 so the error may be in the transfer or calculation of one of the balances in the trial balance.

Test 5

£	2,121	Credit balance

Test 6

Account name	Amount £	Debit ✓	Credit ✓
(a) Bank	3,250		✓
SLCA	2,350	✓	
Suspense account	900	✓	
Bank	3,250	✓	
SLCA	3,250		✓
(b) Suspense account	1,000	✓	
Discounts allowed	1,000		✓
(c) Discounts received	450		✓
PLCA	450	✓	
PLCA	450	✓	
Discounts received	450		✓
(d) Suspense	1,088	✓	
PLCA	1,088		✓
PLCA	1,088	✓	
Purchases returns	1,088		✓

Suspense account

	£		£
(a) Bank	900	Balance b/d (184,266 – 181,278)	2,988
(b) Discounts allowed	1,000		
(d) PLCA	1,088		
	2,988		2,988

Test 7

(a)

Account name	Amount £	Debit ✓	Credit ✓
Suspense	9,247	✓	

(b)

Error in the general ledger	Error disclosed by the trial balance ✓	Error NOT disclosed by the trial balance ✓
Calculating the balance on a ledger account incorrectly by £100	✓	
Recording a supplier's credit note for £800 at £80 in the purchases returns day book		✓
Forgetting to include the £200 balance on the petty cash book in the trial balance	✓	
Making the debit entry for a cash sale of £150 but not the credit entry	✓	
Failing to record a petty cash purchase of food for £20 (no VAT)		✓
For a purchase of stationery on credit, debiting the PLCA and crediting the stationery account		✓

Test 8

(a) (i)

Account name	Amount £	Debit ✓	Credit ✓
Purchases	4,945		✓

(ii)

Account name	Amount £	Debit ✓	Credit ✓
Purchases	3,945	✓	

(iii)

Account name	Amount £	Debit ✓	Credit ✓
Suspense	1,000	✓	

(b) (i)

Account name	Amount £	Debit ✓	Credit ✓
Purchases	980	✓	
Purchases ledger control	980		✓

(ii)

Account name	Amount £	Debit ✓	Credit ✓
Purchases	980	✓	
Purchases ledger control	980		✓

Test 9

Purchases

Details	Amount £	Details	Amount £
		Suspense	256

Motor expenses

Details	Amount £	Details	Amount £
Suspense	893		

Suspense

Details	Amount £	Details	Amount £
Balance b/d	637	Motor expenses	893
Purchases	256		

Discounts received

Details	Amount £	Details	Amount £
		Discounts allowed	149

Discounts allowed

Details	Amount £	Details	Amount £
Discounts received	149		

Test 10

	Balances extracted on 31 March £	Balances at 1 April Debit £	Credit £
Machinery	52,910	52,910	
Fixtures and fittings	17,835	17,835	
Computers	9,920	9,920	
Cash at bank	2,367	2,367	
Petty cash	250	250	
Sales ledger control	115,438	115,438	
Purchases ledger control	34,290		35,618
VAT owing to HM Revenue and Customs	2,337		2,337
Capital	52,254		52,254
Sales	270,256		270,256
Purchases	78,309	78,309	
Purchases returns	3,203		3,203
Wages	54,219	54,219	
Maintenance expenses	3,445	3,445	
Administration expenses	10,254	10,254	
Marketing expenses	6,287	6,287	
Premises expenses	15,244	15,244	
Discounts received	4,278		4,278
Discounts allowed	1,288	1,468	
Totals		367,946	367,946

CHAPTER 6   The banking system

Test 1

	True ✓	False ✓
A bank draft cannot be cancelled once it has been issued	✓	
Any customer who pays with a debit card is taking out a loan with its bank as a result		✓

INDEX

Notes

Notes

Notes

Notes

Notes

REVIEW FORM

How have you used this Text?
(Tick one box only)

☐ Home study

☐ On a course_____

☐ Other _____

Why did you decide to purchase this Text? *(Tick one box only)*

☐ Have used BPP Texts in the past

☐ Recommendation by friend/colleague

☐ Recommendation by a college lecturer

☐ Saw advertising

☐ Other _____

During the past six months do you recall seeing/receiving either of the following?
(Tick as many boxes as are relevant)

☐ Our advertisement in Accounting Technician

☐ Our Publishing Catalogue

Which (if any) aspects of our advertising do you think are useful?
(Tick as many boxes as are relevant)

☐ Prices and publication dates of new editions

☐ Information on Text content

☐ Details of our free online offering

☐ None of the above

Your ratings, comments and suggestions would be appreciated on the following areas of this Text.

	Very useful	Useful	Not useful
Introductory section	☐	☐	☐
Quality of explanations	☐	☐	☐
How it works	☐	☐	☐
Chapter tasks	☐	☐	☐
Chapter overviews	☐	☐	☐
Test your learning	☐	☐	☐
Index	☐	☐	☐

	Excellent	Good	Adequate	Poor
Overall opinion of this Text	☐	☐	☐	☐

Do you intend to continue using BPP Products? ☐ Yes ☐ No

Please note any further comments and suggestions/errors on the reverse of this page. Please send your comments to: ianblackmore@bpp.com

Please return to: Ian Blackmore, AAT Range Manager, BPP Learning Media Ltd, FREEPOST, London, W12 8BR.

REVIEW FORM (continued)

TELL US WHAT YOU THINK

Please note any further comments and suggestions/errors below